PRAISE FOR SUE TABASHNIK'S BOOK

ADVANCE PRAISE FOR *PATRICK SWAYZE Still Inspiring!*

"It is inspiring for filmmakers like me that a great lady like Sue can keep the flame of Patrick's light alive as a beacon for the generations of actors yet to come. We must back her in her quest to keep the greatness of Patrick relevant in today's cynical world."

—*Joshua Sinclair, Friend and Colleague of Patrick Swayze, Director, Writer, Producer, Physician*

"Thanks to Sue Tabashnik, the memory of someone as beautiful inside and out as Patrick Swayze will never fade. You have given us all a gift to cherish and hold dear for years to come. I'm inspired. Let's go Swayze!!"

—*Timothy Linh Bui, Friend and Colleague of Patrick Swayze, Director, Writer, Producer*

Patsy Swayze: Every Day, A Chance to Dance

"I can't tell you how much fun I had reading your book. What great memories I had with Patsy. I know Patsy and Patrick—or 'Buddy' as we know him—would be so happy and proud of your book."

—*Jaclyn Smith, Actress, Designer, Entrepreneur, Philanthropist*

"Your book traces the experiences of the talented artists who were milestones in Patsy's life and therefore in Patrick's life. Above all, you trace the rise of Patrick's career and his love for dance and acting and how it was impacted by his mother and mentor, Patsy."

—*Joshua Sinclair, Friend and Colleague of Patrick Swayze, Director, Writer, Producer, Physician*

"Her many achievements have never been fully assembled in one place and celebrated before. . . . *Patsy Swayze: Every Day, A Chance to Dance* represents a key piece of literature. It should become a mainstay in any performing arts or memoir collection."

—*Diane Donovan, Editor, Donovan's Literary Services*

"Patsy was the first one to integrate the world of dance for African Americans in the city of Houston, Texas. . . . This is an important book for students because they will learn about the history of African Americans in the world of dance."

—*Dwight Baxter, Former Student of Patsy Swayze, Choreographer, Director, and Broadway Performer*

PATRICK SWAYZE The Dreamer

"It's a wonderful journey into the hopes, dreams, and sufferings of a great man. Throughout the book you show how Patrick fashioned his own life to conform with his spirituality and undying hope and resilience."

—*Joshua Sinclair, Director, Writer, Producer, Physician*

"Any Patrick Swayze fan will find this a wonderfully detailed account of not just his life events, but his personality, ideals, and the experiences of a woman who came to document his world."

—*D. Donovan, Senior Reviewer, Midwest Book Review*

The Fans' Love Story ENCORE: How the Movie DIRTY DANCING Captured the Hearts of Millions!

"A celebratory text packed with behind-the-scenes information on the producers, stars, and film team that includes an in-depth interview from producer Linda Gottlieb about its making, interviews and photos with story consultant and dancer Jackie Horner, and more. . . ."

—*D. Donovan, Senior eBook Reviewer, MBR*

"Just fabulous. Love you—love the book. I now will cherish it and all of our memories."

—*Jackie Horner, Story Consultant,* Dirty Dancing

The Fans' Love Story: How the Movie DIRTY DANCING Captured the Hearts of Millions!

"Your book is both great journalism and original writing. It is a very positive testament to Patrick and his life as an Artist and the impact it had on others."

—*Joshua Sinclair, Director, Writer, Producer, Physician*

"The interviews with the people involved in the film are fantastic and give a rare glimpse into the world of *Dirty Dancing* and the Catskills."

—*Jan Griffith*

PATRICK SWAYZE
Still Inspiring!

ALSO BY SUE TABASHNIK

The Fans' Love Story:
How the Movie DIRTY DANCING *Captured the Hearts of Millions!*

The Fans' Love Story ENCORE:
How the Movie DIRTY DANCING *Captured the Hearts of Millions!*

PATRICK SWAYZE *The Dreamer*

Patsy Swayze: Every Day, A Chance to Dance

PATRICK SWAYZE
Still Inspiring!

SUE TABASHNIK

PASSION
SPIRIT
DREAMS
PRESS

Walled Lake, Michigan

PATRICK SWAYZE Still Inspiring!

Copyright © 2024 by Sue Tabashnik. All rights reserved.

www.likedirtydancing.com

The views and opinions expressed and the information alleged by the contributors, interviewees, and other third-party sources in this book are not necessarily those of the author, and the author accepts no responsibility for inaccuracies or omissions by contributors, or interviewees, or other third-party sources. This book is for informational purposes only, and the author makes no representations or warranties, and disclaims any liability, with respect to any information, commentary, analysis, and opinions contained in this book.

This book may not be reproduced, transmitted, or stored in whole or in part by any means, including graphic, electronic, or mechanical, without the express written consent of the author.

This book is an independent publication and not associated with the Patrick Swayze estate.

ISBN 978-0-9894086-8-4 (paperback)

ISBN 978-0-9894086-9-1 (ebook)

PRINTED IN THE UNITED STATES OF AMERICA

FRONT COVER PHOTO CREDIT: Jonathan Exley/Contour by Getty Images.
Patrick Swayze riding horse, posed at a portrait session in 1990.

Book and cover design: Patricia Bacall, www.bacallcreative.com

Editors: Pamela Cangioli and Kimberley Jace, proofedtoperfection.wordpress.com

To my parents, Phyllis and David
To my brothers, Bruce and David
Always in my heart!

ACKNOWLEDGMENT OF GRATITUDE

To Frank Ochberg, MD,
Thank you for teaching me about meaning and inspiration.

ACKNOWLEDGMENT OF GRATITUDE

To Mr. Don Frazier,
Thank you for being my "big brother" and my dear friend for so many years. I will remember your "never-give-up warrior spirit" and carry you in my heart always. Be at peace.

ACKNOWLEDGMENT OF GRATITUDE

To Mr. Patrick Swayze,
Know that you continue to inspire and make a difference in so many lives.

CONTENTS

Overture   1

One CURTAIN RAISERS   3

    Joshua Sinclair   4
    Eleanor Bergstein   5
    Linda Gottlieb   6
    Jaclyn Smith   6
    Timothy Linh Bui   7
    Jordan Brady   15
    Vincent Angell   15
    Christopher Riordan   18
    Terri Garber   19
    Marshall Teague   22
    BoJesse Christopher   22
    Larry Ward   23
    Frank Whiteley   24

Two ACTION: ON THE SET   27

    Jeff Healey as interviewed by Steve Newton   29
    John Philbin   30
    BoJesse Christopher   39
    Bruce Morrow ("Cousin Brucie")   48
    Denise Amirante   49
    Bill EuDaly   56
    Melissa Perry   65
    Scott Wilder   70

Tom Sanders	71
Ray Cottingham	72
Patrick Youngblood talks about Frances and Sam Youngblood	73
Amy Osborn and Joe Cervantez	77
Michael Porterfield	82
Mike Hammond	84
Glenn Watkins	90

Three ALL ABOUT DANCE — 105

Christopher Riordan	107
Dwight Baxter	117

Four SUPPORTING CAST — 122

Rachel M. Leon	122
Larry Ward	123
Michael Pascoe	136
Vicki Mancuso	140
Nancy Schmidt	142
Francie Mendenhall	143
Heather Sparacino Crane	144
Katherin Kovin-Pacino	146

Five **THE FILM CRITIC AND THE ENTERTAINMENT JOURNALIST**   **147**

    Joe Leydon   147

    Alex Simon   149

Six **THE FANS**   **151**

    Jan Griffith   151

    Crystal L. Berger   154

    Claire Gregan   156

    Regine   159

Seven **MORE ABOUT ARABIAN HORSES: STARRING TAMMEN**   **161**

    Paul Kostial   163

    Lilli Keels   170

Eight **PERFORMANCE NOTES: MORE AMAZING INFORMATION**   **172**

Curtain Closer   175

My Applause   178

Permissions   181

About the Author   187

OVERTURE

When I remember Patrick Swayze, the first thing I think of is not Johnny Castle, the sizzling dance instructor in *Dirty Dancing*; Sam Wheat, the loving spirit in *Ghost*; James Dalton, the Zen bouncer in *Road House*; or Bodhi, the rogue skydiver and surfer in *Point Break*. What comes to mind, first and foremost, is what I hold most dear about Patrick: his strength of character and spirituality that still shine so bright.

This collection of memories, stories, and tributes from colleagues in the entertainment industry, childhood and lifelong friends, Arabian horse enthusiasts, and fans is a homage to a man who not only was an immensely talented performer, but who also was a hero. Patrick has left a legacy of many works, including movies, television shows, Broadway shows, dance performances, and songs. Most important is that he lived a life in which he demonstrated courage in the face of adversity—time and time again—and showcased traditional values and beliefs such as loyalty, morality, and integrity. He was an advocate for dance and the performing arts, conservation, cancer diagnostic and treatment advances, and Arabian horses. He battled pancreatic cancer with his "never-give-up" determination, courage, and grace that has touched countless lives.

In the course of speaking with and receiving written material from many of Patrick's professional colleagues, including writers, directors, producers, actors, and stunt staff, a wonderful thing happened. These contributors not only reminisced about their working relationship and friendship with Patrick, but also provided fascinating and exclusive behind-the-scenes information. The contributions from friends and fans are priceless. I cannot thank enough all of the contributors for their heartfelt memories, stories, tributes, and photos.

My wish is that this collection of intimate reminiscences from colleagues, friends, and fans will help preserve Patrick's legacy, and bring joy and comfort to people who greatly miss him and who want to celebrate his life and work. We can use Patrick's way of dealing with the death of a loved one to deal with his death. We can find some kind of meaning and pay tribute to his spirit.

I hope you enjoy this homage to Patrick. It is a contribution to the phenomenal legacy of a man who continues to entertain and inspire millions. In the world that we live in today, it is wonderful to have this hero motivate us to become better people and to make a difference in the world.

NOTES: First, the contributor's affiliation with Patrick is listed after each contributor's name. Thus, by no means is this a complete listing of the participant's work and accomplishments.

Second, the order of the participants was difficult to decide and does not reflect the importance of each contribution, as each one is very special.

In *Chapter One: Curtain Raisers,* I began primarily with the writers, directors, and producers, along with several actors and friends, to give the reader a glimpse of the great variety of fascinating interviews and tributes that will follow.

Chapter Two: Action on the Set showcases the actors, stunt staff, extras, and ancillary personnel.

The additional chapters include participants from the world of dance, friends, professional entertainment writers, fans, and Arabian horse enthusiasts, along with a fun facts section. Finally, Patrick's meaningful and timeless words from multiple media interviews open each chapter.

CHAPTER 1

CURTAIN RAISERS

"No matter how much you prepare yourself for success—you can *never* prepare yourself for it," Swayze said. "Things come up that you didn't know were there. And with Lisa and I, our biggest focus has been, we don't want any of this stuff to change us. We want to stay the kind of people we believe ourselves to be. And try to grow and become better human beings.

I want to keep grounded in the things I believe in, those ideals that sometimes in Hollywood seem a little naïve and innocent. I don't care—I believe in integrity, and a certain level of quality in your life."

Patrick Swayze, December 19, 1988, From Joe Leydon interview

"But I really am hellbent to see how far I can take this craft of acting....

My battle is, 'Can I be the kind of actor that I want to be?' I don't care how you try to box me in. I'm going to break your picture of me. And it's going to be fun doing it. Every time you think you have me pegged, I'm going to surprise you."

Patrick Swayze, September 3, 1995, From Joe Leydon interview

Sue Tabashnik

JOSHUA SINCLAIR

Writer, Director, Producer of *Jump!* Friend

Written by Joshua Sinclair: January 18, 2017

Patrick fashioned his own life to conform with his spirituality and undying hope and resilience.

***Joshua: This is what I said at the LA Jewish Film Festival (2009) when we opened the Festival with* JUMP!**

I have been fortunate enough to work with many wonderful filmmakers in my career. Some you may have heard of, others not. But they are all exceptional and timeless in their art. Vittorio De Sica, Sofia Loren, Roberto Rossellini and young Isabella, Richard Burton, Romy Schneider, Richard Harris, Trevor Howard, Kim Novak, Marlene Dietrich, David Bowie, Sean Penn, Martin Sheen, Karen Allen, Grace Jones, and even Tony Curtis at the end of his Billy Wilder heyday. And I am not just name-dropping, unless it is to drop this one name: Patrick Swayze. Patrick was *Truth*. The cowboy's need to survive at its purest. There was always palpable truth in his emotions, even against the backdrop of Hollywood's lies, deceptions, hypocrisy, and false myths. Patrick was and will remain forever a genuine myth because he represented the humanity inherent in show business distilled to its essence.

In all my career, I have never met such a dedicated and passionate human being—on and off the set. And that is refreshing, to say the least. Patrick Swayze was that sort of miracle that comes along only once or twice in any given generation. It was my privilege to have loved him, to still love him now. Oscar Wilde once said, "We are all in the sewer but some of us are looking at the stars." Patrick was always looking at the stars, no matter what cards life had dealt him. And for that, I thank you Patrick—for your inspiration, for being a hymn to life. Some say we have lost Patrick. I say, no we haven't. I know exactly where he is.

NOTE: Jump! is the 2007 Joshua Sinclair film that is the true story of the acclaimed celebrity photographer Philippe Halsman with a focus on his murder trial in 1928 in Austria. Patrick was awarded Best International Actor for his portrayal of Richard Pressburger, a Jewish attorney who defended and helped Halsman fight against the rampant anti-Semitism of the time.

Bonnie Siegler, in her *Woman's World* article "Patrick Swayze Movies: Celebrating the Charismatic Star's Most Iconic Roles" (November 14, 2023), reports Patrick said he thought *Jump!* was his most important movie.

ELEANOR BERGSTEIN

Writer, Co-Producer of *Dirty Dancing*, Friend

Written by Eleanor Bergstein: April 1, 2017

People have said many fine things about Patrick when he was alive and in tributes later. All the fine things said were true. But I'm sorry I didn't speak up. I didn't want to intrude as the family and friends and fans gave all their most-deserved accolades. But now I would like to say that Patrick was my loyal friend, my collaborator, from the moment I met him he was dear and close to my heart.

But the thing that was singular and most impressive to me about him—and needs saying, again and again—was that Patrick was a very good man. It was the thing that was most important to him, to be a fine and good man who spread kindness and honor wherever he went. He did do that with his talent, his courage, his indefatigable desire to be the best he could for himself and bring out the best in others. With his beauty, his grace, and his generosity—it is this that I miss most about him.

LINDA GOTTLIEB
Producer of *Dirty Dancing*, Friend

Telephone Interview: November 17, 2012

This is an excerpt, edited November 4, 2016, from the book *The Fans' Love Story ENCORE: How the Movie DIRTY DANCING Captured the Hearts of Millions!* (2013) by Sue Tabashnik.

Patrick had a really good heart. If he liked you, you were his buddy, his friend. I saw him years later, and he gave me a very warm, loving embrace. He loved animals. Even when we were shooting, he was often on the phone checking about the animals. I think he was happiest back at his ranch.

JACLYN SMITH
Actress, Dance Student of Patsy Swayze, Friend

Telephone Interview: March 9, 2020

These are two excerpts from the book *Patsy Swayze: Every Day, A Chance to Dance* (2022) by Sue Tabashnik. Jaclyn studied dance from Patsy Swayze (Patrick's mother) from around age twelve (1957) to eighteen (1963).

Did you know Patsy throughout her life?

Yes. And I knew her children. Patrick—Buddy, as I knew him. He and Lisa did some contracting at one of my houses here. He was really starting his career and I had already done *Charlie's Angels* and we reconnected. I saw him throughout. . . .

You couldn't have gotten a more beautiful dancer, very masculine, and yet, technically as good as anybody.

Do you have a theory as to why Buddy became the star out of Patsy's five kids?

It's about magic and he had it. I think there was a lot of talent in that family, but I think he was closest to Patsy in stature, body language, and shape. He might have wanted it more, too. It's not always *why*. It's how hard you try and how hard you go after it. She was a disciplinarian with her children and she really pushed them in many directions. Some take that as a springboard to go forward and some stop.

How many people make it to the height that he made it? Very few, very few.

TIMOTHY LINH BUI

Writer and Director of *Green Dragon* and *Powder Blue*, Friend

Telephone Interview: February 1, 2024

In addition to you being the writer and director of the movies *Green Dragon* (2001) and *Powder Blue* (2009), my understanding is that your brother, Tony Bui, was one of the producers of *Green Dragon*.

Correct. We switched roles on *Green Dragon*. He was the director of the Sundance Grand Jury winner, *Three Seasons*.

Is there anything you can share about how you decided to cast Patrick as Sergeant Jim Lance in *Green Dragon*?

When I finished writing that script, I was at the William Morris Agency. I knew I wanted Forest Whitaker. So he was the first actor that the agency set me up with and the first actor who signed on. I had a list of names for the role of Gunnery Sergeant Jim Lance. Swayze wasn't on that list. I was a young filmmaker at the time and Patrick Swayze was a big movie star. So it never even dawned on me to even consider that high. I thought I was just going to make a little indie film, a personal film about my family and what we went through coming to America in 1975 from Viet Nam—our first steps in a new country, being in a refugee camp for months.

How much of *Green Dragon* was what your family experienced?

Green Dragon was partially inspired by my family's experience and also by a collection of many stories.

So at that time, we had an actors' short list, and the names for me were "gettable." And then one day, I got a call from an agent named Nicole David who represented Patrick. She said, "I want you to meet Patrick Swayze." I was like, *Patrick Swayze*!

That's hilarious.

I'm like, wait a minute! To be honest, I was reluctant at first—not about meeting him, but he had so much star power, I thought it would overshadow the personal story I was trying to tell. Forest, I think, told me, "Hey, just keep an open mind. I know Patrick. I think he might be great for this." Forest was the one that kind of helped ease my anxiety a little bit.

For our first meeting, Patrick Swayze invited me to his ranch here, out in the valley. So I am this new, young filmmaker, nervous as hell, going to Patrick Swayze's ranch. The moment I meet him, I see a movie star, because of all the stuff I had seen him in growing up. Of course, I was starstruck at first, but he made me feel very comfortable. He was just so warm and generous.

What I really remember hitting me was his *eyes*. When you're up close and talking to him, and when he looks at you, there's so much emotion and feeling in his eyes. So much compassion, and thought, and intellect—everything. He's a smart, smart man. When he speaks, he's captivating. He's compelling. In that moment, I began to trust that, okay, I think this can work. This wasn't the movie star who was going to overshadow the story. Here's an actor. I just started to talk to him as to: how does he embody this character? So that was my first experience meeting him and how it came about.

What do you think he brought to the film?

There's a scene where he's in the darkroom and he's looking at all of the photos, trying to understand his brother (who died in the war) and connect with the refugees. He's this guy running the camp, and he's just kind of lost. It's a long sequence, but there's no dialogue. It's just on Patrick's face. In that moment, to me, that's the *heartbeat of the film*: the compassion, the guilt, and what the Americans represent to the war. It's one of my favorite scenes in the film.

Wow!

Because a lot of the South Vietnamese, at the time, blamed the Americans for what happened in the war. They blamed the Americans for abandoning them. That's why there's a scene in the film when Thuy, played by the late Hiep Thi Le, learns that the war is over. She blamed the Americans and attacked Jim Lance. It was very important that I find an actor that represents that voice of what America was going through with the war during that time. Patrick brought strength, vulnerability, a sense of guilt, and a deep compassion to the character of Gunnery Sergeant Lance. Looking back, I was blessed to have him in the movie and that it worked out. That's what Patrick brought to that character, that representation—because he is the sole character that represents America to the arriving Vietnamese at the time. And he was just trying to understand what had happened in the war to his brother, and trying to have the compassion and understand what the Vietnamese people were going through and what they had lost—and what America went through during the war.

This is 1975. The war had just ended, while the camp [Pendleton] was happening. The war was officially over while the refugees were in the camp. Not many people know this, but this is still considered one of America's greatest humanitarian efforts.

Ooh!

Yeah.

Patrick's role in the other movie, *Powder Blue,* is so different. Right?

Yeah. After *Green Dragon*, Patrick and I developed a friendship. We used to hang out a lot. I'd come out to the ranch. The one thing he really loved was writing music. We would be down in his music room, under the cellar, a whole music studio. He would just be writing songs. I think he wanted me to try to put some of his songs in *Green Dragon*. He wanted to duplicate the magic of what he did with "She's Like the Wind." [This is a song Patrick co-wrote with Stacy Widelitz originally for the 1984 movie *Grandview, U.S.A.,* but instead the song ended up in *Dirty Dancing* and became a smash hit.]

Oh gosh, what a song!

Yeah. So that was his big passion—not a lot of people know about it. It wasn't just something he did for that one movie. He was constantly writing music, probably for his own personal creative outlet. I even introduced him to a hip-hop artist friend of mine, and they actually did a hip-hop version of "She's Like the Wind."

Oh, wow!

It was never released. I don't know what happened, but it was pretty cool. They did a whole re-mix and re-mastered new version with hip-hop.

That would be so cool to hear.

So Patrick and I were friends throughout the years. Of course, I wanted to work with him again on the next ensemble, *Powder Blue*. It was like, "Hey, I've got this really crazy role." He wanted to be a part of it. So that's how we were able to work together again.

Remind me exactly what character he played in *Powder Blue*.

He played a character named Velvet Larry. He was the owner of Wally's Whacksack strip club.

Oh, right.

He was kind of this slimy owner of a strip club. I think we had fun with it. He really got to create the character. He went out and picked the outfit, the hairdo. He wanted to be like a "David Lee Roth-hairdo-looking-kind-of-guy." So a lot of it was his creation. We had fun working on that together.

I'm so glad. I mean, that was his last movie, right? After *Powder Blue*, he did *The Beast*, the TV miniseries. But I think your movie was the last movie.

I think so.

I remember the day I got the call. We were going to do a PSA together. I was directing a PSA for a campaign called "Save Burma." I sent the pitch to him and he wanted to do it. I remember I was in the production office with one of the producers. We're waiting for him to call us back. You know, are you in or are you out? Oh, there's Patrick, he's calling me now. He said,

"Tim, I want to let you know something. I can't do it, and here's the reason why. I want to tell you this before it breaks in the press. I have cancer." I was like, "Oh, my God."

Oh, wow! Heavy.

I remember that day. I can never forget it.

So you guys stayed friends, right?

Yeah, we stayed friends. When he was ill, I would come up to his ranch and just hang out and do the music thing. He loved playing his music. My hip-hop friend, Antoneus Maximus, got to know Patrick. We would go up there and chill, and just spend hours in his music studio.

That's cool.

You shared a memory from *Green Dragon* about the photos. Are there any other memories from either of the movies or other stories about Patrick?

One day on the set of *Green Dragon*, he didn't agree with the dialogue that's on the page. We had a little bit of creative difference on it. I will always remember this moment. I'm like, "Buddy/Patrick, you have to say it the way it's written because of this, this, this, and this." He was like, "Yeah, but . . ." He had his reasons. And we butted heads. At the end of the day, he gave in. He was upset. He was like, "Fine, I'm an actor. I don't agree with this, but I can make anything sound good." I remember he said that to me.

But that wasn't the funny part. The funny part was right after he said that, he hops on his little electric scooter. It wasn't prevalent—not everyone had one. So he said that to me, he huffs and puffs, and then gets on the scooter and rides off. Like he rides off into the sunset, huffing and puffing. "God damn it! Okay, you want it, I'll do it!" He was not happy.

I heard about him having an electric scooter on another set, *Waking Up in Reno*. [I also read he had an electric scooter on the set of *Donnie Darko*.]

The scooter helped him get around on set. When we were shooting at Camp Pendleton, it was like being in a studio—it was like being on the back lot of Universal Studios.

In *Dirty Dancing*, he never wanted to say, "Nobody puts Baby in the corner."

I know, and then it became the iconic line, right?

Yeah. These things are really fascinating to me. I hope they will be for readers, too.

Absolutely. You learn things. There's so many behind-the-scenes moments that people don't know about in the course of someone's relationship or the relationship of making a movie together.

I have learned so much on this project.

He was the most down-to-earth guy. I'm sure you know that from other people, and you met him.

Yes.

He was that guy. I remember times he would call me to come up to his ranch. We would drive to the airport. He was a pilot. We would get in his plane and he would just fly to Santa Barbara, we'd have lunch, and fly back. He was such a sweet, nice person. I definitely miss him because we weren't just professional collaborators, we became friends.

This may sound trite, but I'm glad you had that time to do that—although not as much time as would have been wanted by both of you.
    And about the music, I've read that people want to hear his unpublished music. I don't think that's going to happen, though.

You know, in the hip-hop world, they use the term "Swayze" as some kind of slang.

Yes. [According to Elliott Sharp who wrote "Patrick Swayze: The Lost Tapes" published April 11, 2013 on *VICE.com*, "Swayze" became a catch word after the release of the movie *Ghost*. At least seven rappers—Kool G Rap, Method Man, Dres, Nas, The Notorious B.I.G., EPMD, and Young Jeezy—used "Swayze" in their lyrics instead of "I'm ghost," which meant "I'm leaving," "I'm out of here."]
    I wonder what Patrick thought about that.

Yeah.

Is there anything else that you want to add?

The great memory that I can say is near the very end, I went to one of Patrick's get-together parties. I forgot what the occasion was. He was already deep with this illness. We were at the ranch; family and very close friends. Obviously, when you look at him at that time, you're heartbroken inside, but you can't show it. You have to act normal, like nothing's happening. You can't say, "Hey, are you okay?" It's way beyond that. What's great was his positivity, his energy. You wouldn't know he had cancer. If you just closed your eyes and heard him that day, you wouldn't know it. He was still the life of the party. He was going around making sure everyone's having a good time, talking to everyone. It was great. And that, I think, embodies a lot of who he is as a human being, in my opinion.

Yes. That's amazing.

I remember being at Sundance with *Green Dragon*. Back then, I came up with such a big entourage of friends, supporters, and filmmakers. Going from party to party can be very difficult when you have a group of ten people. You can't always get all your family and friends in. I remember, we never had a problem—because of Patrick. At one party, I was at the door trying to get everyone in and then I see Patrick on the second-floor balcony, staring down, screaming down at the bouncers, "That whole group is with me. Let them in!"

That's hysterical.

I remember those nice moments with him. He cared for everybody, which is wonderful.

Was *Green Dragon* your first movie that went to Sundance?

No, a few years before was a film called *Three Seasons*. I produced *Three Seasons*. My brother, Tony, directed it. That's why this year at Sundance I was back there, because Sundance just re-screened *Three Seasons* for the twenty-fifth anniversary.

Congratulations.

When I was out there, my brother was there, my cousin was there. We were talking about, "Remember that photo we took with Swayze right here?"

That day, I saw your text [about doing an interview] and I thought, "Whoa, this is weird."

Yeah. When I got your message, it was wow! What else would you like to share about Patrick?

My childhood film that exemplifies my teenage years growing up in America was *The Outsiders* [the 1983 movie based on the 1967 novel by S. E. Hinton.] I'm a Vietnamese kid growing up in America, and when I watched that film, I just was so connected to it.

Why do you think you were so connected to it?

Looking at that now, I can clearly see it. I didn't know at the time. The film is about outsiders. I'm an outsider. I'm a refugee kid, kind of lost, trying to find my place in the world. People were making fun of me because I was Vietnamese at the time.

Aw.

That's what was happening to the Greasers [in the movie]. And that's great storytelling, if a Vietnamese kid like me can watch that film and identify with it. Later on, how amazing the world works—that many years later, I'm directing Patrick Swayze. It's just like, "What?" I'm so starstruck on my way driving to his ranch: *This is the actor from* The Outsiders, *the film that meant everything to me growing up. How is this possible?*

The Outsiders was one of his breakthrough performances, and I think along with *North and South*, that got him on the map.

That's very interesting that you asked me why I felt connected to that film. I've seen it a hundred times. I saw it in the theaters the first couple times. My parents owned a video store. When it came out on video, it was one of the cassettes that I took home and kept.

Wow. Did you ever talk to Patrick about *The Outsiders*?

I think I did, when I first met him at his home, without sounding too much like a fanboy. "I loved you in *The Outsiders*." That's probably about it.

Yes.

I never thought about it. No one has ever asked me why I connected with that movie. I wish I could have told him that I connected because I was an outsider.

JORDAN BRADY
Director, *Waking Up in Reno*

Patrick was a dear man, extremely humble and funny. Few reach his level of global fame as he did, and still stay so grounded.

Written by Jordan Brady: September 18, 2016

Patrick was always—and I mean, *always*—keeping the energy and humor up on set. But on one particularly stressful day, an hour after he was wrapped, Patrick rode up to set on his electric scooter, wearing a bathrobe, a long redneck wig, and buck teeth. He circled the crew a few times and then disappeared. His timing was perfect! We all had a laugh and were recharged to finish our work.

Excerpt is from the 2000 Official Patrick Swayze International Fan Club interview of Jordan Brady about Waking Up in Reno *[2002].*

VINCENT ANGELL
Creator, Writer, Executive Producer of *The Beast*

Email Interview: January 2, 2024

I understand that William Rotko and you were the creators of the 2009 TV series *The Beast* and that you were also one of the main writers and co-executive producer. Is this correct?

Yes, this is correct. I had a writing partner, William Rotko. Together, he and I came up with the idea for the show. We pitched the idea to several networks, ultimately selling it to A&E. We wrote the script and the next step was to wait to be greenlit to make a pilot episode. That happened at the end of 2007.

Were there other actors under consideration for the role of Charles Barker [FBI agent]?

We did have a phone conversation with Kenneth Branagh, but he passed on the project. Patrick was next on the list, and we were thrilled when he decided to do our show.

What did you think Patrick could bring to the role of Charles Barker?

We thought Patrick would be an interesting choice because most of the characters Patrick had played up to that point were leading-man heroes. Charles Barker was a little more gray—he had a dark side. Charles Barker would often cross lines if it meant getting the bad guy. We hoped it would feel unexpected, coming from Patrick, and it would keep the audience on its toes.

So the pilot gets done and then you guys find out Patrick has been diagnosed with pancreatic cancer. What made you guys decide to take a risk on Patrick to do the series?

We shot the pilot in January in Chicago. Over the holiday season is when Patrick was diagnosed. I can't remember when—but it was shortly into that new year that Patrick invited us to his home, he told us he had news to share. When Bill Rotko, Cory Concoff (a producer on the show), and myself drove to his house, we never expected for the news to be that he had cancer.

We were all so stunned and heartbroken for Patrick. We got on the phone with the studio and the network and let them know what was happening; they were our partners, after all.

Patrick had some treatments ahead of him, so the decision on the show was put on hold while Patrick went through a round of chemo. After a few months, he was healthy enough to get to work. But he still had a battle ahead of him. During production, he was still being treated. He would get his second round of chemo on Friday nights, be sick all weekend, and then show up at work Monday morning. It was amazing to watch this man take on this challenge, to fight this fight, and he had the whole cast and crew in his corner.

As far as taking a risk on him—you're right, that's exactly what it was—a risk. I'm pretty sure on this point, but you might want to fact-check this. It was my understanding that the studio couldn't insure him because of his diagnosis. All actors get insured in case anything happens. It protects the production. They [allegedly] couldn't insure Patrick, but they went ahead anyway. It was almost a gesture to this Hollywood legend. I remember someone from the studio saying, "If we're only able to finish three episodes, we get three episodes, but let's give it a shot."

What do you think are the positives that Patrick brought to his character Barker?

So many. Mostly, his dry sense of humor. It was one of my favorite qualities about Barker. He had a quip for every occasion.

What was it like to work with Patrick on *The Beast*?

It was an amazing experience. I was working with an actor I grew up watching. He was in some of my favorite films, and now I got to write for him and collaborate with him. I was thrilled. And it was a unique experience. We all knew the fight he had on his hands, and it brought us all closer together. Most crews become like family—you spend so many hours together. But it was even more on this project, because of Patrick's battle.

Is there any particular memory or story while shooting *The Beast* with Patrick that comes to mind that you would like to share?

I remember there was a monologue in the pilot that I wrote. And when I was sitting behind the monitors watching Patrick bring to life the words that I had written—I was ecstatic. It was a surreal experience that I won't soon forget.

Did Patrick do all of his own stunts on *The Beast*?

I remember early on, maybe after Patrick read the second or third episode, he called us and he was upset. He thought we were writing less-challenging scripts to protect him. This particular episode wasn't stunt-heavy. It's just the way the episode turned out, but it had nothing to do with protecting Patrick. He was eager and willing to do everything. And we tried to accommodate that at first. He did a lot in the beginning—running and jumping and some amazing stunt driving. But as the season wore on, so did the effects of his chemo, and eventually we had to tone things down. And he had to let his stunt double do a little more—which he *hated*.

How do you remember Patrick?

Fondly. So glad I got to spend that time with him. It was a big break for me as a writer, and to go on that journey with an actor that I so respected made it all the more memorable. It was probably a little over a year of my life from start to finish, but it had such a profound effect on me.

Make each day count.

CHRISTOPHER RIORDAN

Dancer, Actor, Choreographer, Director, Friend of Patrick and Patsy Swayze

Telephone Interview: May 27, 2023

I know you were very close with Patsy [Patrick's mother], and she was a dear friend. I'm assuming that you met Patsy before you met Patrick.

Yes.

Okay. So for some backstory, please tell me how you met Patsy.

We both were members of an organization called the Professional Dancers Society. I became the chairman of the board of directors. . . .

Every year, the organization for dancers used to give an award luncheon to somebody deserving. This one particular time, I think they asked if Patrick would come along. Patsy said, "I'm hesitant to ask Patrick because right at this particular time . . ." It was when he became really, really hot. So she said, "I am afraid people will swamp him. Sometimes these things get a little crazy. You know, some of these people will start grabbing at you and so forth." I said, "Patsy, why don't you take a table next to my table? My son is coming. My son Sean is taller than I am, so he's a bit formidable, and we can watch out for

Patrick." So that's how I met Patrick, at that particular luncheon.

Oh, wow.

I saw him many times after that. . . .

I would see Patrick and his wife at certain functions, you know, Hollywood functions. Of course, he was always just very gracious. It seemed like he always remembered that I had volunteered to protect him….You didn't think of him as being this Hollywood sex symbol. I've known Hollywood celebrities practically my whole life. So it didn't surprise me that he was really a very down-to-earth person, especially knowing Patsy. You couldn't get any more down-to-earth than Patsy Swayze.

Please see Chapter Three for the entire interview.

TERRI GARBER

Actor (Ashton Main), *North and South*

Telephone Interview: July 17, 2023

I'm collecting stories, memories, and tributes to honor Patrick. Do you have any special memories from on the set of *North and South* [1985]?

I can remember he actually taught me how to "dirty dance" before he did *Dirty Dancing*.

No way!

Yeah. After shooting all day, a bunch of us would get together. We'd go have dinner at a place—most of the time we went to Poogan's Porch [in Charleston]. And then afterwards, we'd go dancing. It was just total chaos and fun and we were dancing. Patrick was like, "Okay, I'm going to teach you how to dance with me." I said, "Okay. Great."

Oh, wow.

He taught me how to "dirty dance."

That's amazing.

Yeah, that was pretty cool.

It's hard to talk about him in a way that is like funny stories, because we hung out every day. We were friends. It's not hard in terms of telling privacies—that's not it. It's just there was nothing like special. We would all just hang. We would have dinner every night. We would go dancing every night. On the weekend, we would go to New Orleans.

We were shooting my last scene (I think in the first part), where he hauls off and he slaps me while the barn is burning. We had discussed it beforehand, and there are ways of doing a stage slap, but I was young, and I said, "Just really haul off. We can get a realistic reaction." And he did. I am telling you, one take, he literally knocked me off of my feet. And my hoop skirt went over my head.

Oh, no.

And there I was with my pantaloons and my crinolines all hanging out with the hoop. I couldn't get up. I'm stuck on the ground. He was just great. We had a great chemistry, a terrific way of working with each other. We got the right take. It was good.

Oh, wow. That is quite a story. You said you were quite young. Do you mind saying what your age was while filming?

I was twenty-five.

So what year was that?

1985.

So Patrick was thirty-three.

He was great.

There was an April Fool's joke that Kirstie Allie and I were going to pull on Patrick and James [Read]. It was that a bunch of guys on motorcycles offered to give us a ride, and we said, "Yes." And they took us somewhere and we don't know where we are. And Patrick got so upset and James got so upset. And then we said, "Hah, hah, hah. April Fools!"

I think Patrick was one to pull pranks on sets. I don't know about on

North and South.

He really didn't.

Maybe because of the gravity of the situation and it was such a big role for him.

How long did you film for Books One and Two?

It took about a year with like a month in between shooting, but then we had to come back to have costumes fitted and stuff like that. There really wasn't a lot of time in between.

That's a long time to be on a project.

We were going back and forth. We didn't shoot every day. We shot like some of our stuff on certain days. Some days we didn't work, so we had three days together. I lived in New York, so I could fly back to New York. Patrick's wife, Lisa, came out and she stayed for a while.

Did Patrick's dogs come to the location?

No, the dogs did not come.

I've read and I've heard Patrick do interviews where he talked about how the role of Orry Main just fit him so well, and in a way, he really felt like he fit in better in those times than in modern times.

That's interesting.

That's sort of not surprising to me that he felt that way.

Then I've read stuff about him talking about the costumes, how hot it was and how hard it was.

It was incredible. It was so hot. You would just be drenched. We didn't skimp on what we were wearing. We had to wear everything period, so that was stockings, pantaloons, crinolines, hoop skirt, a dress that weighed thirty pounds, boots, corsets, and a camisole. Everything, every day. There wasn't any moment when we weren't dressed fully.

MARSHALL TEAGUE
Actor (Jimmy), *Road House*, Friend

Written by Marshall Teague: March 5, 2017

Working with Patrick Swayze on *Road House*, I had no idea at the time that I would end up with a friendship that transcended as strong as a brotherly love . . . In my acting career, I've had the pleasure of working with some incredible actors. Many of which I have developed wonderful friendships and bonds. Patrick and I connected on another level. We met as actors on the stage to engage in raw brutal combat; both sharing a martial arts, athletic background. As we rehearsed the fight scenes, we knew we could elevate the realistic intensity as we developed a choreography which turned the physical contact of this fight into a dance. End result, we created one of the best contact action fight scenes on film and a deep friendship for life.

Patrick was a special man. I miss him every day.

BOJESSE CHRISTOPHER
Actor (Grommet), *Point Break*, Friend

Telephone Interview: December 20, 2023

So we go into the table-read finally and everyone's sitting around the table. Swayze's in there and he's got *the Bodhi look*. He's got this really cool kind of character thing. I'm looking at him and I'm going: I'm a surfer. I *know* guys like this. This guy really is transforming. I'm like marveling at this guy. I go *wow*, it's Patrick Swayze, but also, I'm a surfer and I'm looking at the authenticity of what this guy is doing. I feel like this is a guy I know. He's like a guy that I would have grown up with, that was like a mentor. So he's already there for me, character-wise, and I'm just observing this.

Then all of a sudden, he throws his feet up on to the table—in front of like twenty other people. It's those bare feet that I saw earlier! I just said it, I shouldn't have said it, but I said it. Again, I think I'm like nineteen years old. I said it out loud to all twenty people, "Ah ha! I recognize those feet." Because I'd just seen them, but to everyone else it sounded like I was recognizing Patrick Swayze's feet. So he looked at me and he knew what I meant because he had just walked by me and he remembered that I was on the ground as he walked by. He looks at me: "*You're definitely in this movie. You're definitely my brother. That was awesome.*" It was really an affirming, connective moment. Otherwise, I was like a nineteen-year-old kid sitting around a table full of movie stars and not knowing if I really was going to go along for the ride because it happened so fast. He confirmed to everyone in the room that: *I love this kid. He's got a great attitude. He's funny, but also like he's fearless. This is good. This is going to be fun.* So that's the beginning of the day.

Please see Chapter Two for the entire interview.

LARRY WARD
Lifelong Friend

Telephone Interview: June 2, 2023

When did you first meet Buddy?

It was the summer of '65. I grew up overseas in Egypt. We had just moved back. My dad bought a house. I didn't know anybody and I was on my bicycle on my driveway. Buddy drove by, stopped, and introduced himself. [We were the] same age.

How old were you?

Almost thirteen.

His birthday was in August [1952] and mine was a couple of months later in October. . . .

Do you think his fame changed him at all?

I don't see how it could not, but he tried to stay as level as he could. I'd read these articles in magazines, and I'd call him up, and I go, "Buddy!" He goes, "It's Hollywood." For me, he didn't really change that much. I don't know how that would be for somebody else, since we go back to such an early age. There wasn't much he could do. I was very, very happy for his success.

Another one he did for me. He was going to be at the Houston Livestock Show and Rodeo and sing with the Gatlin brothers. He and Lisa were staying at the Astra Hotel, so he invited me and my wife over. We followed him over to the Astrodome. So we're behind the scenes. I knew he was popular, *but I had no idea how much* until he rode that horse around. [I was] watching all the girls almost die trying to reach over the rails and stuff. I go, "Whoa!" He did his thing.

Please see Chapter Four for the entire interview.

FRANK WHITELEY
Longtime Friend and Bodyguard of Patrick

Excerpts from a telephone interview I did with Frank Whiteley on June 2, 2021 from *Patsy Swayze: Every Day, A Chance to Dance* (2022) by Sue Tabashnik.

You mentioned you came into the picture in the nineties.

Yeah, '91.

So you were his bodyguard and friend from 1991 until he passed.

When I was in Houston for the premiere of *One Last Dance,* Buddy and Patsy got on the fans' tour bus and talked to us for about an hour. We could ask anything we wanted. It was very nice that they would get on our bus and do something like that.

Yeah. You gotta remember that Patrick never forgot where he came from. I think that has a lot to do with his mom's influence.

We were in Atlanta, Georgia and we were filming *Black Dog* [1998] outside of a little tiny town. There was probably a hundred residents who lived in that town. We got cut around 2:30 in the afternoon and there were a couple of people who wanted autographs, so he met with them. The line grew to the point where it started getting dark outside. The residents brought food (dinner) out. This parking lot became a giant picnic. They turned on the headlights. We were there until eleven, eleven-thirty at night, just talking with people.

That's the type of person he was. He was very inviting to everybody. He wanted to know what people thought and why you thought that way. It wasn't from a judgmental point, it was from: *I want to know about you.* He was genuinely that way.

I don't think that you find too many celebrities or stars who would do that. Not that I ever became a fan of anybody like this. I wonder what it was like for you, being the bodyguard and friend and watching all these things, like the story you were just telling me about the filming of *Black Dog*.

With Buddy, I enjoyed working with him because not only did we have a professional relationship, but we also had a personal relationship. We enjoyed talking about adventures and camping, whatever it would be, from a spiritual level to, you know, just two boys kicking it.

One of the things that we talked about a few years before he knew he had cancer was, and this started around seven o'clock at night in his kitchen and we didn't end until about 4:30 in the morning.

Oh, my word.

Oh yeah, our conversations went forever. . . .

He firmly believed that with all of his training and knowledge that he obtained over his whole career, that all this instilled something in him, that he felt he had a bigger purpose in life than just being a movie star. We talked about: "*Well, look at all of the people's lives that you have touched with just the movies that you did.*"

"Your mom pushed you in directions that you would never have gone, had it not been for her driving force. So what is it that you're supposed to do?"

Then he passed. I think that he's touched many people's lives. You never know. We talked about that; we just don't know how you influenced somebody's life and made a big difference in it.

He certainly influenced my life. I have a friend, Joshua Sinclair. He wrote and directed the movie *Jump!* [2007]. It was the second-to-last movie Buddy did. I asked Joshua if he thought Buddy realized how many lives he had touched and Joshua thought he did. So I was happy to know that.

Yeah, he knew that. He wished he had more time. He wished he had a kid. That was his biggest struggle in all of his life was that he personally felt he should have been a dad. He learned a lot from his dad. He learned a lot from his mom. He knew what things he wanted to teach and how he wanted to be a father. Our parents teach us things and then we learn from them and then we teach our children similar values, but a different teaching step. He had learned that from his mom. He struggled with that constantly. Different roles would come up and he would shy away from them, like *Father Hood* [1993]. He needed it, and it was a good script, but it brought in his "demons," as he called them. The things that scare you in life, those are demons. He wanted a kid, and it just didn't work.

CHAPTER 2

ACTION: ON THE SET

Patrick was talking about almost being killed while filming *Letters from a Killer* [1998] after his horse ran into an oak tree.

"What saved me was I grabbed two handfuls of his [the horse's] mane, so I'd break my legs rather than go head first into the tree." (He commented that he did break both of his legs and detached four tendons from his shoulder.)

"After I hit that oak tree, it just flipped a light switch inside of me. You know, I mean, I really should be dead, and I'm not. It made me realize I'm on borrowed time. We only have so much time, so you might as well get on with it. I've got a lot I want to say as an actor and as well as a filmmaker and I'm going to say it. The only way to do it is do my projects."

Patrick Swayze, 1998, From Bobbie Wygant interview

Patrick was talking about his wonderful experience working with Gene Hackman on *Uncommon Valor* [1983] and how he wanted to be like him on set with other actors.

"I come from a place where I want to be part of a collaborative, nurturing kind of energy."

Patrick Swayze, June 2004, From Alex Simon interview

Patrick: This is my keepsake [holds up an emerald-and-crystal-encrusted scepter]. It's my magic wand. It has been in the hands of holy men in India and Japan and all over the world. I put it in each person's hand and say this to bless the production and create an atmosphere of mutual goals devoid of ego.

Tom O'Neill: Um, Patrick, do you ever worry about how all the spiritual stuff, like the wands, might affect your image—both inside the studios and out?

Patrick: I don't care what image I have! Take any image you want of me, I'm going to change it, because we are chameleons. We have the crazy person, the shy person, the angry person, the intellectual person, the ignorant person, the gay person, we have the little boy in us, the little girl in us . . . Oh! Heaven forbid we have a feminine side! I've now ceased to worry about image, because I don't care what people think of me anymore. Because I've had such a battle with what I think of me and with trying to find a way to like myself.

Patrick Swayze, September 1995, From Tom O'Neill Us Weekly *interview*

PATRICK SWAYZE Still Inspiring!

JEFF HEALEY

Actor (Cody), Singer, Musician *Road House*

Interviewed by **STEVE NEWTON**
"That Time I Asked 22-Year-Old Jeff Healey what
Patrick Swayze was like to work with on *Road House*"
Originally published July 1, 1988 by Steve Newton in Earofnewt.com

JEFF HEALEY: "He's a marvellous individual. He really is. I think seeing as he's just sort of newly become a star-type figure, he still doesn't know quite how to relate to it all. He's a very easy person to work with, and very humble. Just a nice guy, overall. A lot of fun."

During this interview, Jeff told Steve that his band played about twelve songs in the movie. It was also noted that Jeff had a major speaking part as Cody, a good friend to Swayze's character Dalton.

These two famous lines from *Road House* [1989] show the friendly relationship of these two characters, who obviously had met previously.

Dalton (Patrick): "So, you play pretty good for a blind white boy."
Cody (Jeff): "Yeah, and I thought you'd be bigger."

Cody was not the only character in the film who made that same comment. The owner of the bar Frank Tilghman (Kevin Tighe) and Elizabeth Clay (Kelly Lynch) said the same thing.

NOTE: Jeff Healey—March 25, 1966–March 2, 2008—was a Canadian music icon who was a blues, rock, and jazz guitarist, and a singer, songwriter, and producer. He was also an advocate for the blind and for children with a rare form of eye cancer, retinoblastoma, which had caused Jeff to become blind in early childhood.

Sue Tabashnik

JOHN PHILBIN

Actor (Nathanial), *Point Break* and Actor (Cowboy), *Grandview, U.S.A.*, Friend

Telephone Interview: January 11, 2024

So you were in two movies with Patrick: *Point Break* [1991] and *Grandview, U. S. A.* [1984].
How did you get cast in *Point Break*?

I'll never know for sure, exactly why. *Point Break* was named *Riders on the Storm* originally and the director was Tony Scott. I read for Tony Scott to play Bodhi, which was Buddy's/Patrick's role. I read very well and I was kind of hot at the time. And he liked me. He called me back. So I read again in his office with him. He offered me the role of Nathanial after my reading. At the time, it was a really good, juicy role. I was so stoked because I'm a surfer (since age twelve).

I read that you were a surfer. That is so cool.

I had been in a surf movie called *North Shore* [1987] which I had gotten a lot of heat for. I think a lot of people who were looking for surfers definitely knew who I was and they were like *wow*, this is an actor that can really surf, he can really play a surfer. I don't know if Tony saw that or if it had anything to do with it. I'll never know. My readings for Bodhi were really good and as a result of that, I got the role of Nathanial for *Riders on the Storm* with Tony Scott. But then, the studio dropped the film and it went to turnaround. I thought it was going to be the second studio film where I surfed and got to ride the pipeline and played a surfer. I was so happy. I thought my life was made when I got that. Then it went into turnaround and I went, "Something else will come around." I just kept working. I was working on *Dillinger* [1991] playing a bank robber out in the Midwest somewhere for a TV movie with Mark Harmon.

Then I got a call from my agent saying, "Hey, that movie that you cast in as Nathanial has been picked up by Largo Studios, a different studio. We have a different director now. It's a woman. Her name is Kathryn Bigelow. We have a different cast." In the original movie, Charlie Sheen was cast as Johnny Utah.

Oh, I didn't know that. Wow!

Yeah. Charlie Sheen was going to play Keanu Reeves' role. Sheen was really hot at the time. He was an athlete and an actor. He had done a lot of really good work. He was ready to elevate up, you know, level up.

I was offered the role of Nathanial by Kathryn Bigelow and Largo Studios for this new film. Some of the producers had stayed with the film and they said, "We've already done this work. We cast this guy and he's perfect for it. Let's cast him again and lock it down." I heard that news and I was like: *This is great.*

They sent me the script and I read it. I said, "Who is in it?" The roles this time are going to be played by Patrick Swayze—he is going to play Bodhi and Keanu Reeves is going to play Johnny Utah. They didn't have a title when we started. They might have been calling it . . . I don't know what they were calling it. If it wasn't *Riders on the Storm*, it was *Johnny Utah* or something. It wasn't *Point Break* yet.

And I said, "Yes. This makes my life complete." I read the script and my part was quite a bit shorter. I was a little disappointed, but I was still so thrilled.

It had a great camera department, the Petermans. I grew up in Palos Verdes and I knew this Keith Peterman and Don Peterman, his dad, and they were going to be the cinematographers. They were just an epic family. They were just great. I had always wanted to work with them.

Everything was great. I even volunteered to go and read for it. My agent's like, "You don't have to read for it. You got the part." "No, I want to meet. I want to meet." I flew back in to LA. I showed her all the pictures of me surfing pipeline and jumping out of airplanes. I told her I was robbing banks in Milwaukee at the time, playing this part [in *Dillinger*].

This is a sentence that Patrick Swayze used to tell me. He used to say to directors, "I was born to play this part."

Oh!

And it was great!

I'm not a very good office reader, so I almost read myself right out of a part. But anyway, I was thrilled. Kathryn Bigelow—I did a little research—was a visionary director. She was an artist at the time and, as it turns out in hindsight, a genius because she looked at Keanu Reeves in *Bill & Ted's Excellent Adventure* [1989] and said, "I think this guy can be an action hero with a gun in his hand and command the same amount of attention as the biggest movie star in the world, Patrick Swayze." Studio executives were like, "What do you mean—that stoned kid in *Bill & Ted's Excellent Adventure*? And Patrick Swayze in *Road House*?" She was like, "I think he [Reeves] can do it." As it turns out, she was right about him.

And Patrick Swayze to play a surfer: He was a cowboy. He was a ballet dancer. He was an incredibly romantic dancer, movie star. But at the time, *Ghost* had not come out. So he was like, "Okay, I'll do this low budget, independent film that is being cast with a guy from *Bill & Ted's Excellent Adventure*. I like the script that Peter Illiff wrote and so I'll do it." They were lucky to get him.

When I met him in the read-through, I was like I had worked with him before. I'm like, "Yeah Buddy, *Grandview, U.S.A.*" We had that work experience in common.

He became *my everything*: my hero, my leader, my Bodhi. I mean, he took care of us. He took us into his family.

That's so sweet!

Before the film finished shooting, *Ghost* [1990] came out. Patrick Swayze became the biggest movie star in the world, again. He had been there before, but he wasn't at the time, and then during the filming, it came out. We're like, "Oh my God, we've got the biggest movie star in the world in this movie, Patrick Swayze, doing an incredible job." So we were pretty excited. That's how I got cast.

That's awesome!
Are there certain things you remember about shooting the film?

Yes. I remember we rehearsed a lot.

Patrick Swayze would pass the wand around, his magic wand.

I read about his wand. [See beginning of this chapter for more information.]

He's a very generous man. He's very loving and he wants everybody to succeed. He used to take us in his Range Rover; he used to drive us up to Arrowhead. The bank robbers, we became like a little group: James Le Gros and sometimes BoJesse Christopher—just us, no one else—not the Razorheads. He would take our gang up to his house, let us sleep in his Arrowhead house, and then we would drive to Perris and skydive with him. And then he'd drive us back to Los Angeles. We'd be like, "Wow, man." He did that a bunch of times. He took us water skiing on his lake in Arrowhead. He brought us to his ranch where he had Arabian horses and Lisa was there. He would talk to the horses and kiss their noses and they loved him. This guy's just letting us in on his life. He was very down-to-earth.

In fact, I will say a story that is bad for me and good for him.

On the set, I was very much in character, a lot of the time, but half in character and half just myself—an actor, you know. I came up after lunch and I met the boys. We're in the makeup trailer. "Hey, have you ever been out on the set, just kind of walking around talking to people? You strike up a conversation. You're talking to someone for a while, and you're just talking to a couple of guys and they say something to you that reminds you that they are an extra." Patrick goes, "Why, do you think you're better than them?" I'm like, oh my God, it hurt my heart so much.

He is not about anybody feeling superior to anybody. *He's very much like a working-class hero kind of guy*. Even though he's a huge movie star, he loves just the normal people. There's no elitism in him and he was the biggest movie star in the world. If he even smelled someone might be entitled or elitist or in any way feel superior to anybody else, he would fight for justice for anybody. I saw that in him then. I was embarrassed. It's not what I meant at all. Extras have a certain way of talking about the job that actors don't. It's very easy for me to forget I'm on a movie set when I'm in character. I didn't mean it the way he thought it. But it made me realize what a hero he is: he's a real guy's guy.

Also, he couldn't go anywhere without women [being around him]. We'd be robbing a bank [in the movie]. If he was on the street, cars would stop and he'd have to put his mask on or go inside. We wouldn't get anything done because people wanted to be near him, and see him and say hi to him, and tell him how much he meant to them in their lives.

Those were stories that happened during the filming.

Which president did you play in the movie? Was it Carter?

Carter.

About how old were you when you were in that movie?

I would say thirty years old.

How do you compare that experience of *Point Break* to the earlier movie you were in with Patrick?

The first movie I was in with Patrick was *Grandview, U.S.A.* He played a tough guy—demolition derby, a guy who was in love with Jennifer Jason Leigh and Jamie Lee Curtis at the same time. He wasn't playing the smartest guy in the room. He was playing a tough guy, but he had a heart. He was sensitive.

I was playing a mentally challenged person. We just said hi to each other a couple of times on the set. I was in character the whole time. So I was hard to talk to as just an actor from LA. He didn't need to do that to be brilliant. Patrick Swayze's a movie star. This is not a big part. He wasn't the lead of this movie.

I had seen him in *The Outsiders* [1983]. I was a fan because of his physicality. I just thought he had a special physicality that I wanted. So when I would go and talk to him when I wasn't in character—we'd be off the set somewhere. I would just kind of talk to him about stuff I admired as a fan. It was the first movie that I ever got cast in. I was brand new to the business, and here I am with Patrick Swayze, Jamie Lee Curtis, Jennifer Jason Leigh, and Tommy Howell. It helped that I was in character all the time, so I wouldn't be intimidated seeing them on the set.

But off the set, I would ask Patrick questions about *The Outsiders*. He was so cool. He had worked with Tommy Howell on *The Outsiders* and now they're doing *Grandview, U.S.A.* Randal Kleiser directed *Grandview, U.S.A.* and also *Blue Lagoon, Grease, Flight of the Navigator, and White Fang*. He was like a huge director and made hits. He had the cast of all these superstars in it [*Grandview, U.S.A.*]—some of them before they were superstars and some of them after. Troy Donahue and Carole Cook were in it. It was the coolest cast—group of actors, I've probably ever been in, besides *Tombstone*.

Patrick was so generous. He talked about his experience on *The Outsiders*. It was eye-opening for me because I realized that movies don't always come out to be what they start out to be. I was like, wow, that's interesting.

Coppola hit the ball out of the park [with *The Outsiders*]. It was a huge movie for everybody.

Yeah, it sure was. I saw that. I hate to admit it, but the other movie, *Grandview, U.S.A.*—I never watched it. I should watch it.

Oh yeah, definitely.

I don't know how I missed out on watching that one. I've probably seen almost all of the rest of Patrick's movies.

That's funny. *Grandview, U.S.A.* was the first movie I ever got cast in out of college. I was so excited. I was playing a mentally handicapped guy. I was going to be working with all of these movie stars. It was my first job.

Before I went to film that movie with Patrick and Jamie Lee Curtis, I got another job, a little horror movie called *Children of the Corn* [1984]. I'm like, it's a small part, but you know, it's a good part—I'm featured. My agent said, "Yeah, you do this little horror movie. It's low budget and you have a small part. Stephen King wrote the short story, but he didn't write the screenplay. It's a super-small studio. You can learn how to work in front of the camera: learn about lights, and sets, and marks—how to work. So when you go do your really important, Academy Award- winning movie that's going to change the world, *Grandview, U.S.A.*, you'll be ready." I'm like, "Yeah, yeah! Okay." So I did this little horror movie. I didn't know how to work in front of the camera. I got some experience with Fritz Kiersch, the director. I played my little part, Amos, in *Children of the Corn*, thinking no one's ever going to see it. As soon as I wrapped that, I went to the location Pontiac, Illinois to shoot the movie that was going to change my life and make me a household name, with all of these other household names. It was going to be a big deal.

Forty years later, I'm going to fly to about eight different states and do these horror movie conventions where I just sit for hours and meet fans for a movie called *Children of the Corn* which became a cult classic. My picture is on their bodies from that movie and nobody, including you, nobody saw *Grandview, U.S.A.,* the serious, important movie that was going to change the world. So that's just another example of how you never know when you make a movie, what's going to happen with it—if it's going to find its audience or if anyone's going to see it. You might think it's the greatest movie in the world. But if nobody responds, who cares? If you think some movie is just not that important, no one's going to see it, and it goes on to win a fan base and becomes relevant forty years later. I get paid more in a day to sign autographs for *Children of the Corn* than I did for making the entire film. That just gives you an example of how strange and how unexpected [it is]; you cannot predict how a movie is going to live in the world.

Point Break is such a cult classic.

That's another good example. Here's a movie that when it opened, it kind of got panned. People weren't sure what to make of it. Surfers were like "eh," they didn't know. Then ten years later, people are naming their children Bodhi and their dogs Bodhi. Dead presidents' shirts are all over the world right now. [The bank robbers in *Point Break* wore face masks of former presidents.] People think they're cool. When they surf, they're wearing dead presidents' shirts. Surf companies are picking up the dead presidents—this is thirty years later—as a brand. It's hysterical!

Keanu Reeves has become the hugest movie star on the planet, just like Patrick was, and that was his first action film. Now people just look at him, and some people go, "He's Neo," some people go, "He's John Wick," but a lot of people go, *"He's Johnny Utah"* because that movie has legs.

It grew into this cult movie for some reason. You never know *why*. I would say Kathryn Bigelow (the director), Keanu Reeves, Patrick Swayze, plus all the background actors. You don't know what's going to happen with a movie. You're just doing your best, playing it for real. And as it turns out, people just ended up loving it.

Had you done skydiving before you did *Point Break*?

I jumped out of one airplane with a static line in California City when I was in college at USC. When I got the role in *Point Break,* Patrick was training by skydiving and he invited us to go skydiving with him and we said, "Yes." I'll just speak for myself. I just said, "Yes" and I went with him. I joined the accelerated free-fall course and I jumped eight times with him.

Then we jumped in Hawaii. All of the surfing took place in Hawaii. We went to the North Shore of Oahu and they've got a skydiving field and I jumped with him by myself in Hawaii. That was really wonderful because in Hawaii, when you jump out of an airplane, you're looking at the horizon and the horizon is blue. The blue ocean meets the blue sky. There's nothing scary about it. When you jump in Perris Valley, you're looking at the horizon that is covered in smog and the ground is brown, flat, dusty, and rocky. You're like, that just doesn't look enticing to me. But in Hawaii, you're just looking at the ocean.

So you have a lot of good memories with Patrick.

I have nothing but good memories. After the movie, Patrick would call us and stay friends. He would call us at night and talk to us for hours. He shared what he was going through. It didn't end with *Point Break*. He continued to love us because there was something about that movie I think he loved. He knew we loved him and he loved us. He was just an amazing man.

When I worked with him, he would go a hundred percent in every take, sometimes even all-in on rehearsals. And that's not normal.

He was a really good athlete. He was scary to play football against, I'll say that.

Really.

Even if you were on camera, he was throwing full body blocks. I'm like, he's going to break my leg rehearsing for a football scene! Let's just fake the contact. He just goes all-in.

He was maybe heading toward a football career before his knee injury [while a senior in high school]. At least, that's what you read.

He was an incredible football player in our football scene. He was scary.

I wish I could have seen him dance, too. You know, his mother had a dance/ballet thing in Houston, Texas. I wish I could have seen him dance when he was younger. That would have been great.

Yeah. I actually wrote a book about his mom—that was my last book. I was just fascinated. She was like an unbelievable person, too. She was very athletic and she was hundred percent all-in, with an incredible work ethic.

That makes total sense that his mom was amazing.

So the filming of *Point Break* took a while?

Yeah—ten weeks—not including Hawaii, and they had to go back to Oregon for re-shoots.

What else, when you think about Patrick? Any other stories?

There was a time when he didn't want to drink anymore and I don't drink—I'm sober. He called me with some questions about what that lifestyle is like. He did some research into that. He was so famous—he couldn't just go to a 12-Step Alcoholics Anonymous program.

No, he couldn't.

In fact, he would attract a lot of attention. I'd see him sometimes with his baseball cap pulled down and his cool little fanny pack where he kept his Parliament cigarettes.

He was just curious about it like: *How's this work? What's this all about?* I shared as much with him as I could.

He was just so friendly to me and just so kind to me. He valued my opinion. I was like, *Dude, you're the biggest movie star in the world, what are you asking me for?* He was just super-cool.

It just sounds like it didn't go to his head—being so famous.

Yeah, it did not go to his head—whether it was the training in dance or football or whatever. Being a movie star did not go to his head. He just treated everybody the same. He was just a real hero for the common man.

Yes. I met him four times as a fan—at two screenings of the movie *One Last Dance* [2003] and two benefits for Complexions Contemporary Ballet. He treated his fans great.

Yep.

We were in Nashville at a film festival [where *One Last Dance* was

shown]. He did a Q&A and afterwards everyone wanted his autograph. He's giving all of these autographs. His bodyguards were saying, "Come on Patrick, we have to go." "No, no. I have to finish giving these autographs."

Right.

It was so cute.

    Wasn't it around the time of *Point Break* that he got the "Sexiest Man Alive" title from *People magazine*?

Yeah, probably.

Regarding getting the "Sexiest Man Alive," Patrick was flattered, but according to several sources, he also did not take the award too seriously. Actually, in several interviews, Patrick talked about Sean Connery being the sexiest man in the world. Patrick's mother, Patsy, was quoted in *People* [August 1991] as sharing that Patrick doesn't think he should be considered an idol—that he just thought of himself as a regular Texas kid.

Yeah, for sure. He never played the idol card, ever.

Right. I just think he has left an incredible legacy.

Yes, he has. I'm glad you are writing a book about him.

BOJESSE CHRISTOPHER

Actor (Grommet), *Point Break*, Friend

Phone Interview: December 20, 2023

For a little backstory, how did you get cast for *Point Break*?

I would love to share that with you. Let's definitely start there because that really ignites the beautiful experience I had getting to know Patrick Swayze.

The movie was called *Riders on the Storm*. Peter Illiff, who we both know and love, wrote this beautiful script. It was called *Riders on the Storm* based on the Doors' song.

A friend of mine, an actor Brian Austin Green, who is famous for *Beverly Hills 90210*—he got the audition for this role of Grommet, the role I ended up with in the movie *Point Break*. We were really good friends and we were hanging out. He said, "Hey man, I've got this audition at the end of the day. It's about surfers who rob banks. I know that you're a surfer. I don't really understand the dialogue. Can you warm me up with this? Maybe drive me to my audition and just kind of warm me up to the dialogue, the way these guys speak to each other?"

I said, "Sure. That sounds fun." So Brian gave me his keys. I get his truck and I'm driving him across town to his audition. We're running lines back and forth and I'm memorizing this stuff, because I'm basically coaching him on this role—inadvertently.

We get to the audition. It's the last appointment of the day for this role. Apparently, they can't find an actor they really like. They're considering offering it to Jake Busey because Gary Busey is in the movie. They're like okay, if we can't find the kid, we'll just give it to Gary's son, Jake Busey.

Oh!

Nobody knew this because it's kind of behind-the-scenes. So Brian goes into his audition. I'm sitting in the waiting room on the floor. I've got the long blonde hair and I've got the cool, kind of surfer look because I am a surfer, born and raised in northern California. So I had this really cool kind of northern California vibe with the flannel and the beanie with long blonde hair. I looked the role. I was the guy. I was an actor. I was in town to do the acting, but this was not my audition.

Brian comes out of the audition and he has this body language about him that I knew: If the audition didn't go well, he would bite his nails. So he came out of the audition biting his nails. I looked at him and I went, "It didn't go well?" He's like, "No bro, let's go. Let's get out of here." He was kind of like in a hurry to get out of there for some reason. He was holding the paper, the scene. That's one of those things that every actor wants to try to accomplish is memorization before you go into an audition, because you get in your head when you have to look back and forth to the paper.

So long story short is, the casting director follows him out, this gentleman Rick Pagano, and he looks at me, and I'm sitting on the ground. And he goes, "Are you next?" I said, "No." He goes, "Are you an actor?" I said, "Yes." And he goes, "You're next." He saw something he really liked. So I stood up. I didn't even think about it and walked right past Brian. I remember Brian, looking at me going: *Bro, you can't do that, that's not cool.* I just walked right past him. I had his car keys in my pocket, so he had to sit there and wait for me.

I got into the casting room. Rick Pagano, the casting director, looks at me and he goes, "Let me hand you some sides, the selected scene from the script." I said, "No, that's okay. I think I got it. I think I have it." So he looks at me kind of like: *You think you got it? Oh, let's see what you do. You're going to bomb just like the last guy did!* So he goes, "Why don't you sit there and let's do the scene." So I stood on the chair instead of sitting. I stood up on top of the chair. I just dove right into what I knew was the monologue. I had this kind of iconic, classic scene at the campfire where I'm talking about dropping into a big wave and the whole thing.

Oh, that was you!

Yeah. So I do the monologue. I've got it committed to memory and I'm a surfer, and it just kind of really flowed.

He looked at me and he goes, "Hold on a second." Then he left the room and he came back with Kathryn Bigelow, the director.

Oh, wow.

He looked at me, and he goes, "Do that again." I'm still standing on the chair. So I do it again. It's beautiful. She looks at me and goes, "You're hired."

I commandeered my good friend Brian Austin Green's audition. It happened organically, but I commandeered it. I won the role in the room, which almost never happens. Then I started work on the film the very next morning.

That is amazing!

So you played Patrick's little brother. Right?

I did, yes. I played Grommet/LBJ. Lyndon Baines Johnson was my ex-president who was robbing banks.

And Patrick was Reagan?

Correct.

Peter said Patrick and you and all the guys lived together while you were filming?

So that was probably basically the time when we were shacked up in Hawaii doing some of the surfing scenes. Patrick had a big, beautiful house on the north shore of Oahu. It was like right in front of the world-famous [surfer's] pipeline. The production rented the house for him. Of course, we all wanted to hang out at the house and be close to Patrick and just have that ocean view. We never lived together, but that was kind of that scenario.

I will tell you some stories.

So the morning after I booked the role, I show up at 7:30 a.m. because we have a scheduled table-read where all the actors were going to get together around a big table and read the script and get acquainted. And then the director would hear everyone bring the characters to life. I got there extra early because I hadn't read the script. I was the last one hired on the film. I'm on the ground again, just kind of hanging out reading the script. I didn't have any time to prepare at all. So I was just like oh, my gosh, I heard there's a bunch of big movie stars. I don't know who is really in it, but here we go. It's a big film. I've just been hired. I did my deal. I'm reading through the script on the ground and I see a person walk by. I look up and I don't really know who they are. I see another person—oh, there's Gary Busey. I see another person—there's Keanu Reeves. Keanu wasn't a big star then, he was kind of coming up, but I recognized him from a few smaller films like *The River's Edge* [1986] and a couple of other movies.

Then I see these bare feet walk by me. This is where the Patrick story kicks in. They're kind of like beat-up surfer feet. I don't really look up because I'm just trying to read the script, but they walk right by me and the script. It was like an insert: my view was the script, me turning pages and then these feet that just kind of traveled through my eye line.

So we go into the table-read finally and everyone's sitting around the table. Swayze's in there and he's got *the Bodhi look*. He's got this really cool kind of character thing. I'm looking at him and I'm going: I'm a surfer. I *know* guys like this. This guy really is transforming. I'm like marveling at this guy. I go *wow*, it's Patrick Swayze! But also, I'm a surfer and I'm looking at the authenticity of what this guy is doing. I feel like this is a guy I know.

He's like a guy that I would have grown up with that was like a mentor. So he's already there for me, character-wise, and I'm just observing this.

Then all of a sudden, he throws his feet up on to the table—in front of like twenty other people. It's those bare feet that I saw earlier! I just said it, I shouldn't have said it, but I said it. Again, I think I'm like nineteen years old. I said it out loud, to all twenty people, "Ah ha! I recognize those feet." Because I'd just seen them, but to everyone else it sounded like I was recognizing Patrick Swayze's feet. So he looked at me and he knew what I meant because he had just walked by me and he remembered that I was on the ground as he walked by. He looks at me: *You're definitely in this movie. You're definitely my brother. That was awesome.*

It was really an affirming, connective moment. Otherwise, I was like a nineteen-year-old kid sitting around a table full of movie stars and not knowing if I really was going to go along for the ride, because it happened so fast. He confirmed to everyone in the room that: *I love this kid. He's got a great attitude. He's funny, but also like he's fearless. This is good. This is going to be fun.* So that's the beginning of the day.

So mid-day, we were all scheduled immediately to go down to the South Bay to Redondo Beach and go surfing with the surf instructor (who has been hired on to the film) to see if I could surf. I was hired, but they really wanted to make sure I could do the surfing portion, which I could. We get down there, and I'm surfing with Patrick Swayze and Keanu Reeves and the rest of the cast. After the surf session, again he gives me the nod: *This kid is the real deal. He's in.* We end up at the house of the surf instructor. It's me, Patrick Swayze, Keanu Reeves, and the other two guys who were bank robbers in the film: John Philbin and James Le Gros. We were all close-knit guys. This is Day One of just prep.

Patrick says to us, "Hey guys, huddle around the TV. I want you to see something." So Patrick pops in a VHS cassette and he shows us the skydiving sequences that he filmed out-of-pocket with his own camera crew, unbeknownst to the production. Apparently, at the time, he was not supposed to be doing that. So it was like very top-secret stuff and he was showing it to us. He says, "Alright. I've been doing this. I'm certified. I'm going to do all of my own stunts, or as much of it as I can that they will allow me to do. I would like for you guys to do it, also." At that point, we all looked at each other and went, "You want us to skydive?" He goes, "Yeah." We all kind of looked at each other and we all agreed at that moment, "Okay. We'll try it." And then we said, "When?" And he goes, "Today, now."

Oh!

So literally, this is all within twenty-four hours of me getting this job.

So then we're off to the desert, to Lancaster, Palm Desert, to go jump out of a plane to get certified to skydive. Pretty much the whole crew. This is Swayze, this ignites the whole kind of like: *When you're around Swayze, this is the kind of stuff that happens.*

We were on the movie *Point Break* for nine months.

I didn't know that.

There was a moment after we all agreed to go skydiving, where Patrick turned to me specifically and said, "Call me Buddy." And I kind of chuckled because I didn't understand what he meant by that. When I call a friend Buddy, it's an endearment, but I didn't know how dear and personal it was to him. And he goes, "It's not funny. Call me Buddy." I said, "Oh, okay. May I ask why?" "Because my dad called me Buddy. I don't go by Patrick. My friends and family call me Buddy."

Wow.

So that's a really clear distinction that most people maybe don't know. He never went by Patrick, he went by Buddy.

Yeah. His dad, I guess, went by Big Buddy.

Yep.

That was cool.

That was fun to find out, because that moment was slightly uncomfortable because I had chuckled, but also it brought us closer because it was a big brother/little brother moment that really pulled my focus in on the sincerity of this guy's heart. I could really see the emotional connection he had with his father and how much that meant for him and that was how he self-identified and felt most comfortable. He represented that in a very protective way. So from that point forward, he was Buddy.

And I loved that about him. Okay, that was beautiful. He shared that with me. He may have had those moments with the other guys, too—but not at that moment. That was my moment.

Wow.

Then we all went skydiving, which was beautiful, and it really brought the bond together.

I remember we were getting a little closer to principal photography. The movie *Ghost* was in the movie theaters at the time. And you remember, *Ghost* was like the biggest movie in the world when it came out.

Yeah.

Patrick Swayze was again the biggest movie star in the world. It was really beautiful work in the movie *Ghost* opposite Demi Moore and Whoopi Goldberg. It was a real tear-jerker, beautiful film. Everyone wanted to get a look at Patrick Swayze if they could, wherever we were on set, and we shot in the South Bay of Los Angeles: Redondo Beach, Hermosa Beach, Manhattan Beach a lot on *Point Break*.

So we were at the beach one day. The public had access to the set, but it was controlled access. So we were entertaining a couple hundred people that were kind of lucky to be able to observe our pre-production. We were throwing a football and we were surfing and doing pre-production stuff. Patrick was giving interviews on the beach to *Entertainment Tonight* and *Access Hollywood* and all of the news outlets because of *Ghost*. Also, this was the new film that he was doing after *Ghost,* and everyone wanted to know: What is this movie you're doing after the success of *Ghost*? I was pretty close to that action. I was maybe twenty feet away. I'd just come in from surfing. . . .

I was the youngest of all these guys. I was Grommet, which is the youngest of the tribe. I was his brother in the film. We had this extra little layer of connection. He really made an extra effort to be there for me in other ways, too.

Patrick would call me every night.

Really!

Every single night. My scheduled phone call was midnight, every night. He was the kind of guy who would call each of the cast members and the director and they all had a scheduled time every day. So I would wait for his call. We would just talk. He was very generous with his time. He would vent to me a little bit about his day. He would share with me some of the things he was feeling. And then he would ask me, "How was your day? How are you feeling?" He would really listen. And then, he would say, "Okay, we're going to do these scenes tomorrow. Can we talk through the scene?" He would give me the scene as good as it possibly could be. Then he would say, "What are your ideas, BoJesse? What do you think would make the scene a little better?" On the other side, he would make notes into the script and I would make notes on my end, too. Whatever we worked out or workshopped on that phone call would literally end up in the movie.

Oh, wow!

It was beautiful because we weren't trying to re-write the script, but what we were doing was trusting that we were these people, and so we were bringing really good ideas to the moment. Then we'd have to pitch those ideas to Kathryn Bigelow, the director, and Peter Illif, the writer, right before we would shoot. Often, it would surprise Peter and Kathryn, because they were not expecting changes that they didn't create. Then we'd have to show them what it looks like, basically. Then, after a little bit of push and pull, most of the time, Kathryn would be agreeable and Peter would say, "Okay, that's great. That really works." A lot of that helped the film overall because it was something that was fluid.

Patrick understood how to make the most out of something, not to just rely on a linear, one-dimensional aspect of filmmaking, but to really get in there and poke and prod and push and pull things until you found the deepest, most meaningful connection to it. He taught me that just by way of doing and showing me it can be done. It has become ingrained in my discipline in all the work that I do as an actor and filmmaker now. It was really a beautiful thing to be a young actor and learn a process and observe his process that was relatively unknown to a young person like me at the time. And I'm learning it from the biggest movie star in the world. Just a beautiful thing!

I can share with you an end-of-life story that's endearing.

Okay.

After I did this movie *Point Break* in 1991, this movie changed my whole career. It opened up all the possibilities and opportunities that one could hope for as a young actor. I stayed in touch with Patrick/Buddy, the entire run of my career.

Probably closer to the end of the nineties, I ran into Buddy at the Sundance Film Festival. I think he had the movie *Donnie Darko* [2001] premiering there. I was producing movies at that time. I remember running into him at one of the parties. Then he and I just linked up and spent the whole night going from one party to the next. It was an impromptu reunion. Everywhere we went, everyone wanted to say hello to Buddy, obviously. But he made a point of saying, "Hey, everyone, you all need to know who this is. This is BoJesse Christopher. He's a hot, young, up-and-coming producer." At the time, I was kind of pivoting into producing films. He really went out of his way to make sure that people at The Sundance Film Festival knew that I was the guy: *If you wanted to get a cool movie made, you come to this guy.* That really made me feel good. We spent six to eight hours together.

We took a really wonderful photograph at the Sundance Film Festival. It was the last photograph that he and I had together. Then I didn't see him again before he passed, but we stayed in touch throughout the years. There were a lot of times where we would check in with each other—have phone calls. There were a few times when I tried to put him in a couple movies that I was producing, and it didn't work out for different reasons, but he had tried to make it happen.

And then when he passed, he had put together a beautiful short list of people (because he was planning for it) that were his, you know . . . He loved everyone, but he had a list of people that he really wanted to be in a room together to memorialize him and pay tribute to his life. I got this wonderful phone call from his wife, Lisa, inviting me to his memorial service. It was curated by Whoopi Goldberg and it had everyone: Bill Paxton, Rob Lowe, Ralph Macchio, Demi Moore, Whoopi, Lori Petty, Kathryn Bigelow, Gary Busey, and me. I mean the list goes on and on, all iconic people he worked with in front of the camera and behind the scenes. It was probably about fifty people. It was a really small group of people, but it was such a wonderful way to say that everyone in this room worked with Buddy in a meaningful way and he remembered it and he wanted us all to celebrate his life in that moment. It was a great way to put a button on that beautiful relationship we each had with him.

This is making me cry.

Yeah. It was really something to be invited to that.

The president of his official international fan club was invited. She and her husband flew in from Europe. It was all top-secret until it was over.

Wow. He was just a generous guy. He was a very passionate, generous, caring person who had a really strong point of view. There was that other side of him: it was like if you crossed that line, sometimes you would feel a little bit of, there's a lion inside this guy. But also there's a big, beautiful heart that cares so much about what is happening that the other side of him wants to protect him. I love that about him. He was very compassionate and understanding, but also if you crossed him in the wrong way, he would let you know. He really would. That never happened with me other than that one time I met him and he said, "Call me Buddy." I caught a little glimpse of it, but he was very gentle about it, because it was our first meeting.

    I love the man. And boy, I sure do miss him.

BRUCE MORROW "COUSIN BRUCIE"

Actor (Magician), Period Music Consultant, *Dirty Dancing*, Broadcaster

Telephone Interview: June 23, 2023

Thank you for agreeing to this interview.

My contact with Patrick was up at Lake Lure. We were shooting *Dirty Dancing* [1987]. I really observed, more than I had contact with him.

    He sort of stayed to himself a little bit. He was absolutely really a nice guy. He was very, very friendly. It was a very busy time. All of us were on our projects and on our shoots.

Is there anything else you may have observed about him from the set?

All I remember really is that when we watched the dailies at night, I remember him sitting there with his two dogs. He flew his dogs in. They were big dogs.

I observed him a couple of times with "Baby" Jennifer Grey. They weren't too friendly. In the pursuing years, I read what had happened.

How did he hurt himself? Was it during the scene when he was on the log over the water?

I don't remember. He told me he hurt himself. He pulled his groin. He had to rest. So they flew the dogs in to give him some comfort. I remember he hurt himself pretty bad.

I wish I could contribute more to you. Let me just reiterate. He seemed to be a lovely guy. He was quiet. He wasn't overly zealous. When he was on the set when we all worked together, he was just a nice guy. He wasn't overly aggressive with anybody. He didn't shove his weight around as a star. He melded in with the company.

My overall impression was positive. He was nice. He was doing his job, and I know he was in pain.

DENISE AMIRANTE

Stuntwoman, *Dirty Dancing*

Telephone Interview: October 14, 2023

Thanks so much for doing this interview.

You're welcome.

How did you happen to get cast in *Dirty Dancing*?

I lived in Queens at the time, in a one-bedroom apartment, and I got a phone call from a stunt coordinator Jim Lovelett. He was referred to me.

He asked me if I was available and interested in doubling a no-name actress in a low-budget movie in the fall. I said, "Sure. I think I'm clear." We talked a little bit and then before we hung the phone up, he gave me the address to the production office to go drop a picture and resume off and meet with some folks. Then he told me the name of the movie was *Dirty Dancing*.

At that moment, actually, my heart sank. I wasn't so sure what I was going to do. About six months earlier, I had accepted Christ as my Lord and Savior, so I thought to myself, *I can't do a movie called* Dirty Dancing. I didn't know how to deal with it. So I thought, I can't tell him the truth and I can't lie. So I decided to just leave it up to God and say, you know what, if this is your will, I'll get it and do it, and if not, I won't get it.

In about a week or two later, I got another phone call and was told that I would be doubling an actress, Jennifer Grey, in the movie.

Had you done stunt work before *Dirty Dancing*?

Yes, I had.

What was your role in the movie?

I was Jennifer Grey's stunt double, meaning I was wigged and wardrobed to look just like her. One of the scenes we did was the car scene when Patrick drove us in the car into the wooded area, and got out of the car, and did a couple of things. Then the other scene, of course, was the log scene, where I doubled Jennifer dancing across the log with Patrick.

There was word that I was supposed to possibly come down to do another scene, but that was never confirmed. I'm thinking the other scene was the water scene, when he lifts her up in the water. I would have loved to have done that scene. I heard from people that the weather didn't cooperate. So that was just scratched. But again, I don't know for sure that they were actually considering me to do that scene.

If we could go back to the car scene, is that the scene where it's raining or is that the scene when they are driving back from The Sheldrake Hotel?

I want to say that it wasn't raining that day, but it was muddy, so I think that was probably the scene. We drove into the woods. I had a raincoat on.

I know they had to fake the rain. At least, that's what someone told me.

Were you at Lake Lure for these scenes?

Yes.

Getting back to the real famous one, the log scene, so what was it like to work with Patrick?

He was very normal. Patrick was very kind. He was a gentleman. He had just come off of doing *North and South*, I believe, a TV series. He wasn't famous yet. So he was just a normal guy doing a role in a movie and very, very nice. I wasn't nervous at all.

So when you're on the log, that line where Patrick says, "Don't look down. Look in my eyes." Was that scripted?

No, that was just he and I on the log. What happened was, I started dancing and he started following me along. There was one moment when we lost our balance. At that point, it wasn't scripted at all. The camera was so far away, it was just a wide-shot of us dancing on the log. This was just he and I talking to each other. He just said, "Don't look down. Look at me in my eyes." So I did and he did and we regained our balance. That's when we just went to the races and started dancing. We had some fun there for a little bit and made it to the end of the log on solid ground.

I will say as a Christian girl, in my real life, I fell very short of what God had called me to do throughout my life. I would have fallen off of that log. But when Patrick said, "Don't look down. Look at me," it was as if I was looking into the eyes of Jesus and getting my balance back, in my life, in the right direction. That was also when, in my real life, things came together for me again with my priorities.

That sounds very amazing, deep.

Yeah, it really helped. It helped me get back on track because I had fallen very short as to what I was called to do.

Did you guys do the scene in one take? Or were their multiple takes?

They had me practice on a balance beam in the dance room for rehearsal. I actually went on the log and I worked with Patrick's stunt double a couple of times. He ended up not being used for the scene. Patrick did his own stunt—just did the scene himself. When Patrick and I did it, we just shot it once.

Oh, wow.

The director thought it was perfect and we never had to do it again. And it's funny because, as a stuntwoman and an actress, you want to do it again, because you think: *Oh that was* so *much fun! Let's do it again, I could do better.* But I didn't have a chance to do it again.

So the story goes, Patrick fell off of the log and had to go to the hospital to have his knee drained. Were you there when he fell?

No. I was not there. I don't know when he fell. I know that when he was on the log before I got on the log to do the scene with him, I was sitting at the end of the log and then I get up and start walking across the log. There was a point where he did a pirouette on the log. I think the director must have said, "Do not do that again because if you hurt yourself, we're in trouble." He was very dynamic that way. He didn't hurt himself while I was there for our scene. I don't know how he hurt himself.

Linda Gottlieb, the producer, told me when I was interviewing her for one of my books, that she had to take him to the hospital. I heard one of the other people in a documentary talking about it, too.

It's so amazing. At first, I never knew that there was a stuntwoman for Jennifer. It's so seamless how they put it together. Did you meet her, too?

Oh yeah, we met. She also was nice. We didn't have a lot of time to talk. But after I got done doing the scene, she came over to me and we were just standing together, and she said, "I can tell you're an actress." And I said, "How?" She said, "Just by the way you work." I guess she was happy with the job I did. I don't know.

Are you still an actress and doing stunts?

No, I'm not doing stunts anymore. I would consider acting. With my book coming out, I was asked to speak at some churches and a couple of places to start sharing my testimony and sharing the book *Don't Look Down: Learning How to Live a Fearless Life by Taking Courageous Steps of Faith and Finding Hope Along the Way*. A lot of times when authors write a book, they go on tour or talk about their book. I think I probably see some of that in my future. Maybe some time next year I'll start doing some of those things. It makes me a little nervous because I have never quite done that. I mean, I've been in front of people before, but I've never quite shared my story on that level. If those are the doors that get opened, then I'm going to walk through them.

Sounds great. Do you want to say something about your book?

My book is about my life from the time I took the call from Jim Lovelett [stunt coordinator for *Dirty Dancing*] to do *Dirty Dancing* to the time I accepted the call to follow Jesus in my life. I use the log scene to go in and out of the log scene of my personal life throughout the book. At the end, I end up on solid ground with Patrick in the movie—and then I end up on solid ground with my faith and Christ. My story goes in and out of the movie and my faith. There are some teachable lessons in there, things that I've learned and how God has brought me through, because I have been through a lot of hard times and I know that I owe it to God that he got me through all of that.

And I've been forgiven for the bad choices that I made in life. I was abused as a child sexually, so it really put me on a bad path. I was very introverted, and quiet, and shy—you know, the self-doubt and self-esteem and the fear gets instilled in a child that young, and that has followed me throughout my life. I've got it under control right now.

That's great. Congratulations on your book!
Did you ever watch *Dirty Dancing* to see yourself or just to see the movie?

Yeah, when it first opened in New York, I went with a friend to see the movie. It was fun to be in the theater and see myself on the log. Nobody knew it was me, but me and her. It was interesting because out of all of the movies I have done, *Dirty Dancing* is the only movie that stayed in the theaters for one total year. I've seen the movie, but I haven't watched the movie that many times, maybe three or four or five times. I'm not one of those people who just can't get enough of *Dirty Dancing*—it never did that to me, maybe just because I was in it.

What an experience, though. This movie is so iconic and you were a part of it.

Yeah, it was exciting.

It was so seamless. At first, like I said, I had no idea that there was a

stuntwoman for Jennifer. I heard some aggravation from other people because Patrick did not use a stuntman and he got hurt. But that was Patrick.

Yeah. If you do look at those scenes now, you'll definitely be able to tell from my wig that it's definitely not Jennifer.

I'll have to look again. I haven't watched the whole thing through in quite a while. I might watch scenes here and there. I find it a little bittersweet, you know, missing Patrick. Not that I was an intimate friend, but as a fan and now as an author. It's so iconic.
 I guess because of the strikes, this production of the sequel of *Dirty Dancing* has been pushed back to maybe 2025 now.

Yeah, I read 2025. It must be challenging for them, because I would think that what they're doing with the movie is not in that time [period], but with the characters being older. Right?

Right. A lot of the actors are no longer here, not just Patrick, but some of the others as well. It's going to be interesting.

Yeah, we'll see.

Jennifer Grey is one of the executive producers of the sequel, and she is going to star in it. They say they are going to do justice to the movie. I read they were in talks with Patrick's estate to somehow incorporate him in there.

They really have to be smart about it.

Some of the other attempts to follow up have not turned out so well. I didn't see the [2017 TV movie] remake, but I was told negative comments and I read negative reviews about it.

I didn't see that either.

***Dirty Dancing: Havana Nights* [2004], the prequel, I think was okay, but it was nothing like *Dirty Dancing*. Patrick made a cameo in it.**

Actually, in December, I'm going to see *Dirty Dancing in Concert* in Nashville. I guess they're touring this year, next year. I don't know what that's going to look like.

I think they may have come to Detroit and I missed it, unfortunately. I remember the original concert tour when they came to the Detroit area, probably in 1987 or 1988. It was totally amazing.

Any other thoughts about Patrick or the movie?

Patrick wasn't a star yet, and neither was Jennifer, and being a low budget movie no one on that set thought that it was going to do what it did. And that's the miracle of it all. That's just the *wow* factor. I would think that Eleanor and Linda were all like: *Can you believe this?*

You said you practiced with Patrick's stuntman a little bit on the log?

Yeah. There were two stuntmen for Patrick: Norman Douglass and Billy Anagnos. I don't remember the name of which stuntman was supposed to double him on the log. I want to say it was Billy. Patrick did all of his own stunts, from what I know.

We [Denise and the stuntman] got on the log because I think in the beginning it wasn't clear that they weren't going to use him. We just got on the log to get a feel of it all. You know what? I think that scene would have totally been different if Patrick's stunt double was used and not Patrick. I'm glad it turned out the way it did.

Me too!

I went to the Madame Tussauds Hollywood wax museum [December 23, 2012]. They chose to remember Patrick by having Patrick on the log. There's nobody on the log with him.

You're kidding.

I was going out to see my dad who lived a couple of hours away from there. Anyway, *it looks so real*. I just couldn't even believe it! It was very startling. I don't like wax museums as a rule, but I sure was going because I was in the area. They have the nature aspect of it around him on the log. It was almost sort of spooky.

Wow, I bet.

Just think of that, how they managed to pick that scene. Out of the whole movie, they picked that one scene.

It's so funny. So many times, when I talk to people about the movie, this is one of their favorite scenes. For me, I love the end scene where they all dance together. That's like one of my favorite moments in any movie. I love dancing in a movie.

Have you been a dancer?

I took dance classes. I was one of the actresses who moved well, but I wouldn't call myself a dancer, dancer.

It's so great that you have the talent to do these kinds of things. Not everyone can do this. Right?

Yeah, I was chosen.

BILL EUDALY

Actor (Tom "Stonewall" Jackson), *North and South*

Telephone Interview: July 27, 2023

Thank you for doing this interview. I found you in the *North and South* Facebook group.

I was flattered that you asked me. This *North and South* thing, only maybe three weeks ago, they contacted me. I had not given it a thought for the longest time. Richard, one of the administrators of the [Facebook] group, asked me if I wanted to join, and I said, "Sure" and he said, "Well, you'd better get ready for this." I said, "Okay." He introduced me in the morning and two hours later, there were two hundred likes and dozens of comments.

Wow.

These folks are just hard-core fans. They even remember my scenes, and some of them remember lines that I had completely forgotten. It means something to them. They're very dedicated fans and they know the whole series intimately, which I don't. I mean, I haven't even seen it in forty years.

I like *North and South* [1985] and I'm happy that I have done it, but it's not something that's an integral part of my life. I've had the best time! It turns out that I had all of these photographs I took and memorabilia, like call sheets, newspaper articles. So I've been posting those. The fans just love it! So it's been a real shot in the arm for me—just a boost, especially at this time while the strike is on for the actors. [From July to November, 2023, the American actors' union SAG-AFTRA was on strike over a labor dispute with movie and television producers.] I also do a lot of volunteer work and consulting with non-profits, but since COVID they have been mostly shut down.

I have lived in Atlanta for many years. My acting stuff—I've worked in NY and the West Coast and travelled. Now about thirty percent of all film production in the country is done here in Atlanta. It's number three, after LA and Vancouver. It's the third largest production center in the US. There are multiple studios. I've worked in some world-class studios here. There's just constant production.

Are you still a social worker?

No, I retired in May 2022 after doing it since 1977. My last job was in an ER for about thirty-four years at a busy hospital on the border of Detroit.

I'm sure you're enjoying your retirement.

Yes, it gives me more time to write—which is my passion.

I know that you played Tom "Stonewall" Jackson in *North and South*. [Jackson was an officer in the Confederate States Army during the Civil War.] I'm collecting stories, memories, and tributes to honor Patrick. What would you like to share from your experiences of working with Patrick on *North and South*?

I've shared a fair amount of anecdotes and pictures on Facebook. I took my 35-millimeter with me and took photos when I could, but I was in a lot of scenes. Somebody took a photo in which Patrick had his shirt off and even though he was sweating, they were putting more sweat on him. It's just a great picture. I may have taken it. The young ladies used to swoon over that one when I was teaching high school, too, at the time. I shared a lot of these pictures with them.

When I got the part, I didn't even know who Patrick was, because in those days before the internet, if you hadn't seen someone in a film, book, or magazine, you didn't know who they were. He was a star, they said—and James Read, too. I didn't meet Patrick until we got to Washington, Mississippi, at Jefferson College that was used for the West Point scenes. It was named for Thomas Jefferson.

I met some of the other actors, the guys that played the other generals, as we were at the same motel. I met Philip Casnoff (who played the part of Elkanah Bent who turns into such a horrible character), but Philip was a very nice guy. They cast everywhere. Mark Moses (Ulysses S. Grant), that was his first film job and he became a very fine actor. Cody Hampton (George Pickett) was from Atlanta and I met him on the plane. And this guy Chris Douridas (George Mc Clellan). They cast in NY, LA, nationally, and here for the part I got.

So I think I met Patrick for the first time during the first scenes, just on the set. He said to call him Buddy. He was very friendly, very outgoing, very engaging. I liked him instantly. I thought he was just the nicest guy.

Just as in life, stars are just like anybody else; they have personalities. I was trained in theater. So I had toured and done a show at the Kennedy Center. I had done several films and worked with some pretty big stars. I was used to working in any kind of environment.

James Read (George Hazard) was very professional and a little more introverted, very nice to work with. Patrick Swayze was very outgoing to all of us who met him. We shook hands and then we started doing some of the scenes, like the bucket scene, one of the first scenes filmed. We were doing those together: firing the rifles, marking, drilling, doing the bucket stuff. Then I had several scenes inside the barracks where we were talking about Elkanah Bent [the sadistic drill master]. I interacted with Patrick in a number of these scenes. He was just very, very good to work with.

What was so good about working with Patrick?

He was very professional and hard-working. What people may not realize is that most stars have to work hard, because the movie depends on them. He was in most of the scenes. We were in and out, sitting at the pool. He was constantly working, so that's very hard. Patrick was just thoroughly professional—giving, listening, everything he did.

It was obvious on first meeting him how athletic he was. He was muscular and had a great build. He had the athleticism and he was also a dancer. That bucket scene was a tough scene to have to go through. I thought that he and James Read did that scene very, very well. Those were my first impressions of him.

In between scenes, we would chat when he had time. I got to know him a little bit and he got to know me. He was very interesting to me. His main preoccupation seemed to be dancing and the film business.

He said that Gene Kelly had been very instrumental in helping him, which is not surprising. Gene Kelly of course, being a muscular, athletic dancer like Patrick was—different than the very elegant, ballroom kind of thing that Fred Astaire did. Patrick said when Lisa and he went to Hollywood, he was helpful. Gene Kelly had seen them in a play. [The play was Patrick and Lisa's 1984 *Without a Word*, which eventually they made into their 2003 movie, *One Last Dance*. There was talk of a possible collaboration in the future.] It sounded like Gene Kelly had been a mentor. Patrick spoke very highly of him. Gene Kelly later was in *North and South* in a cameo [as Senator Charles Edwards].

Yes.

Patrick talked about the importance of treating the crew well, as the crew can be a crucial element in making the film come to life. Sometimes the crew—if they don't like actors, they can mess things up. He said he really believed in respecting the crew, wanted them to feel they were important. He made everybody feel important. I think he had a sense of himself and his personality was genuinely a nice one. Plus, he understood that making everyone feel included is an important ingredient in making a successful film because it's a collaborative effort. Making a film is like an industrial production, as there are hundreds, if not thousands, of people in between every scene. There's all of this preparation in making these brief moments, but that's what makes it look good and makes it work: the costumers, the makeup people, all the technicians, everything. I think he was very, very conscious of that.

One time, our little group of guys went out with Patrick and spent the evening dancing at different clubs. He was just fun to spend the evening with. . . .

We went back to the motel and he was showing us rodeo tricks with his lasso. He had more energy! It was like three o'clock in the morning. I still see him there with his shirt on and his big, bulging arms doing these [rope] tricks, standing there in the little grassy area. That's my last memory of that night.

He signed my copy of the book *North and South*. I had everybody sign it. I need to find it.

I just felt like that whether this was the context we had met in or not, I would have always considered him a nice person, somebody who I respected and liked. I felt he kind of put you at ease. I just have nothing but really, really good memories of him in *North and South*.

Did you guys think *North and South* was going to be as big of a hit, like it turned out to be?

I suspected it was going to be a big hit because that was the days of the miniseries. Back then, there was *The Thornbirds, Roots, Winds of War*, all these mega-hits. I thought it was going to be big, but not as big as it was. I didn't know it was going to command such an audience. *North and South* was right up there. People are still buying and watching it on DVD and YouTube, fans all over the world—Australia, Europe. There is a huge following in Europe. So they all watch it and they just love it to death.

I heard a very cute story that Eleanor Bergstein, who was the writer and co-producer of *Dirty Dancing*, told in an interview. [The interview was in the Extras section of the *20th Anniversary Dirty Dancing Edition*, Lionsgate 2007.] She was flying with Patrick to one of the locations for the movie. They had to go through the airport in Charlottesville. Eleanor wanted to get a hot dog and Patrick wanted to just get on the plane. Patrick ultimately agreed to get the food. So they stopped and then Patrick instantly got mobbed by female fans and Eleanor realized why Patrick had been in such a hurry to get on the plane. As you know, *Dirty Dancing* was filmed after *North and South* (1985) [and Patrick was famous in the South following the TV miniseries].

Lisa, his wife, was with him [on set]. We were introduced. He seemed to be very committed to his marriage.

Patrick mentioned during one of his many interviews that he kept a book for *North and South*. It was sort of almost like a playbook in terms of each scene he was in—what he wanted to get out of the scene and the

character development. I thought that was pretty cool.

I think someone posted something about that on the site. I don't recall it. He was very methodical and very serious. This was a very important, pivotal role for him. He just impressed me as being very professional. I'm sure his training as a dancer and as an athlete probably helped his concentration.

Yes.

You train in various ways as an actor. People have all kinds of methods they use, [and] study with different teachers and different people.

The part of Jackson, I didn't have the chance to develop it much. This was in the days before the internet. I did try to go to libraries to find out what I could from books to at least get some handle on the character. They took a lot of license with it, but I wanted to have it grounded a little bit in reality. George and Orry, of course, were fictional characters. James and Patrick had to just take most of the cues from the script and the context of what was happening.

Is there one photo you have that you might want to share, that you took or a friend took?

I'm in several with Patrick. I would recommend that you go to the Facebook site where I have posted original photos. The bucket scene I posted recently. I know I posted him getting ready to get his diploma. All the photos I posted are originals.

I will tell you a story not about Patrick, but just about me, which shows how precarious the business is. I got that job by the skin of my teeth, less than probably forty-five minutes after I heard of it. Back in those days, again, before the cell phones and texting, I came home and there was a message on my answering machine from my agent: "Bill, I've got an audition for you at 2:20 at Colony Square Hotel for something called *North and South*. It's about the Civil War."

I looked at my clock and it was 2:20 now! So I called the Colony Square and spoke to a person who was working on the auditions, and I was told, "You missed your audition." "But I didn't know about it! I just got home. I only live about ten minutes away, so I can be down there." "Don't bother. You missed it. We're finishing up here. They don't want to see you." "Are you sure about that? I would really love to."

I just had a hunch, and it was about the Civil War, and I'd grown up in the South and knew a lot about the Civil War. So I jumped in my car. I drove to Colony Square. There was this person sitting at a table in the hallway with a bunch of scripts. I said, "Hi, I'm Bill EuDaly." She said, "Oh, I talked to you on the phone. Auditions are over. You should not have come." I said, "I'm sorry."

I walked down the hall and saw this gentleman with a beard: Paul Freeman, one of the producers. He looked at me. His eyes got large. I had a beard. A lot of men weren't wearing beards at the time because they were not fashionable. He came out of the room. He said, "Come here. Amazing. Amazing." Then Chuck McClain [producer] and Richard Heffron [director] came over. They're all looking at me like I'm from Mars. They're going, "Amazing resemblance!" They had a picture of Jackson. They said, "Read this" and handed me a script. I read it, not more than two minutes. They were staring at me.

I started to say what I know about the character, but Richard Heffron reached out his hand and said, "Bill, you're knocking on an open door." I said, "What do you mean?" "You got the part." That's serendipity. That rarely happens. I'm not an aggressive person, but I just wasn't going to take "no" because I had a feeling.

And then, ironically, when I got to Mississippi, they made me shave the beard because the cadets couldn't wear beards at West Point.

That's hilarious. I love that story!

It's one of my favorite stories. I used to tell young people about it. "Assert yourself in the right way and don't let anybody tell you no."

On the way out, I did say to her [the receptionist], "I got the part." She looked at me and her face just dropped and she couldn't believe it.

Then, the next thing was to learn a little bit about Patrick and the other stars. Like I said, I wasn't able to learn that much.

It was a very fun set. We were there maybe three or three-and-a-half weeks. I didn't have any negative experiences. Director Dick Heffron was wonderful, the producers Paul Freeman and Chuck McClain, the crew. It was a positive experience the whole way through.

I'm so glad. You'll always remember it.

Now I look at it and see how much it means to people. This is just so great, to be able to be a part of this. To these folks, it's a big thing in their lives. I love to be able to talk to them.

How big was that cast? Like hundreds of people?

Yeah, I'm sure, hundreds. I have a few call sheets on the principal actors, all of us who had speaking roles, all the way from the top stars down to anyone. They don't list the extras. I know there were a lot of young men playing cadets who were from, I think, Southern Mississippi University. They add so much, but they don't get a lot of credit. It's unfortunate. It's one of the things the strike is trying to address, because they get paid very little and they work hard. They add immeasurably to things. Again, it's like a factory production. It's just so many people involved in these things and the money that is spent to produce these films. It's a huge undertaking.

I'll tell you another funny connection for me. I grew up on a little island in southern Georgia that's beautiful, beyond description. There's an old plantation on half of it. There are some houses that are just spectacular on the river that have been used in a lot of movies (one was *Cape Fear*). In 1973 (when I was in high school and about seventeen years old), I just lived down the street and I would go watch them film *The Last of the Belles,* based on a short story by F. Scott Fitzgerald. It had Richard Chamberlain and Susan Sarandon. I would just go sit on my bike and watch.

Later in my career, I got to be in a miniseries with Richard Chamberlain. (I didn't have a scene with him.) The last thing I did last year was a show called *Monarch* which was on the *Fox Entertainment Network*. Susan Sarandon was in it.

That's amazing.

Both of those people I watched as a kid. I hadn't started acting yet and that was an experience, like a kid in a candy store. It just looked so cool. I got to be in projects that both of them were in.

But anyway, we were there on the *North and South* set three or three-and-a-half weeks. It was a very, very positive experience. Patrick Swayze helped make it that way, among all of the people. Patrick was just especially a lot of fun and a very, very engaging person.

One other thing, you could tell he was a very accomplished horseman. One of the anecdotes somebody shared was that James Read may have gone to Patrick's ranch to ride horses. Patrick did rodeos and he was very accomplished with this.

In some ways, Patrick was like a big kid—that part of his personality was adventurous and playful. And then he had a part that was very, very dedicated. When you talked to him, he didn't just talk about himself. He talked about other people. He was interested in other people and different points of view.

Jean Simmons played Patrick's [Orry's] mother [Clarissa Main]. She was one of the great actresses from the Golden Age of Hollywood. She played Ophelia in Laurence Olivier's *Hamlet* [1948]. She was in tons of movies throughout the forties and fifties. I met her and I was so impressed. She was there in costume some days. I remember just being thrilled to meet her. One of the cool things was people got to meet these big stars and legends. People were just thrilled.

From what I read, Patrick was thrilled to meet some of these big stars and legends, especially one of the male stars. He was really looking forward to their scene together and also, understandably, had some anxiety about it.

Well, it may have been Jimmy Stewart.

Maybe. [After researching, I found out that according to a 2004 Warner Brothers' *North and South* **documentary and Patrick's 2009 autobiography** *The Time of My Life***, it was Jimmy Stewart (who played Miles Colbert in** *North and South***). Per the 2009 autobiography written by Patrick and Lisa, he also felt so lucky to have the cast include Elizabeth Taylor, Olivia de Havilland, Johnny Cash, David Carradine, Lesley-Anne Down, Gene Kelly, Jean Simmons, and many others.]**

When Patrick had his illness, I did write to him. I didn't hear back, but look, I'm sure they had tons and tons of mail.

They did.

And he was probably too ill. I was following that. I knew enough about medicine to know that pancreatic cancer is a bad one. By the time the symptoms show up, it's already too late in many cases. He got some extension, but then passed on. That's really too bad.

MELISSA PERRY

Actor (Brett Main, as a minor), *North and South*

Telephone Interview: August 4, 2023

So how old were you when you were in *North and South*?

I was twelve years old. I only worked two days with Patrick. I didn't have a whole lot of interaction with him, other than little mild sitting around, here and there. I had a few little moments that I can tell you about.

For a little backstory, could you explain what your part was?

I was cast as Brett Main, his [Patrick Swayze's character's] little sister. I was the second Brett, Brett number 2. There was the younger group of the Brett and Ashton [Main] sisters, and then of course, Genie Francis and Terri Garber were the older two sisters.

Stephanie and I were like the middle-school-age Ashton and Brett. I lived in Charleston, which was where they were filming. They came to my middle school and my mom, I guess, caught wind that they were going to be there. I wasn't an actress or anything. I guess they were looking for somebody who resembled Genie Francis as a little girl.

It was kind of one of those weird situations. A strange man came into our lunchroom. We were all eating lunch. He was sitting on the stage and looking at all of us students. Everybody was sort of going up there—being the bold middle-schoolers they were—to talk to him, and I'm the lone kid sitting at the table. They called me over, "He wants to talk to you now." I said, "I need to get my mom. She's working here today substituting." So I read for the part. Another girl who went to my school read for it also. They put me in the role. I only had two lines, so it wasn't a big deal—but it was a big deal to us, of course.

Of course! That's so cool!

Yeah, it was cool.

The first time I met Patrick Swayze, I was in the makeup trailer. They were finishing up my wig and that kind of thing. He came in and looked over and said, "I guess you're my little sister." I didn't know him. I was a kid. I didn't know of his movies, but I knew he was famous. I believe I had met Stephanie and had talked to her, and she was really excited about meeting him.

Was she around your age?

I think she was either twelve or thirteen, maybe just a tad bit older than me. We were both silly—running around giggling, just kind of fast-friends. She gave me the 411 on who exactly he was, since I hadn't seen anything he had done. I was a kid.

He wasn't that well-known at that point—1985.

He had done *Red Dawn* [1984]. Stephanie knew who he was. I don't know if her mom knew, but she knew who he was, and so she was really excited. She thought, as all of the little girls [did]: "Oh, he's so handsome!"

He was very kind. We had these little side-chats, everybody sitting around, goofing off.

He signed my book [*North and South*] for me. I was there for two days.

Stephanie was from Atlanta and she was staying at the hotel where they were all staying. She happened to be down the hall from Patrick Swayze. She was so excited. We went over there to visit with Stephanie and her mom. My mom was giddy, taking pictures of all of us.

We ran and started knocking on his door and harassing him.

Really?

Our moms were like saying, "Don't bother him. Keep the doors shut." We were trying to make him say hi to us. He was very sweet. We saw that he had a picture of his wife [Lisa]—she was on a horse or something like that. We're like, "Who's that?" He said, "That's my wife—the love of my life." [He was] very sweet about that. "You girls better move along. I have stuff to do."

He was very nice. He tolerated our antics. He joked around, just very good-spirited and a good sport, dealing with twelve-year old girls running around.

He was a good guy. So I can see that.

He was really genuine.

And then, I think the second day of filming, they had said, "Meet us at the hotel and ride in the van with us." Meaning, everybody was riding in that little shift of people who needed to go to the set early in the morning. So we met there and I eagerly asked him [Patrick] as soon as I saw him that next morning, "Would you sign my book?" He said, "Let me finish my coffee and my cigarette first." I had the *North and South* book by John Jakes. I was having everybody on the set who we encountered sign it.

I'm sure you still have it—right?

Oh yeah. I still have it. He wrote a little sweet insert that said, "I love you, little sister. Have a great life. Love, Patrick Swayze."

That's sweet.

Everybody signed it. It was really nice. Mitch Ryan. Genie Francis.

Anything else about Patrick?

Like I said, we were really excited to meet him. This was back when one-hour photo had become a thing. My mother and Stephanie's mom were taking pictures of all of us. My mom was running off to one-hour photo and having them developed and bringing them back. We had all these pictures and she had made copies, I guess for Stephanie, and maybe some for us to give to Patrick Swayze. We would take him pictures of all of us together. We would hand them to him, and he would say, "Oh, thank you girls." And he'd give us a little hug. Oh gosh, we have to go back to our moms to get more pictures, so we can get him to talk to us more. It was just funny; little, starstruck girls.

James Read was very kind, too. If I recall, I think they [Patrick and James] had dressing trailers next to each other. We were frequently running around trying to see who was doing what and they were frequently back and forth, sitting around and chatting with each other. On and off the set, they seemed to be very friendly with one another.

That's good.

I think everyone was kind, at least from my perspective.

They had a lot of really big stars in that miniseries—oh my goodness! A lot of them are no longer here.

That's true.

Jean Simmons was very kind. She would sit off on the side. I don't know if she was knitting or doing needlepoint. Mitch Ryan was very kind, very paternal. He would always come over and say nice things to us. I remember I was going to eat and my mom said, "I need you to cover your dress up. You don't want get anything on the dress." Of course, I'm twelve and thinking she doesn't know what she's talking about. So Mitch Ryan said, "Can you cover that dress up?"

That's funny.

My mom looked at him like "Thank you."

What was it like for you with *North and South* being such a big hit? Did you become famous at your school?

I did. Everybody thought it was exciting. In our town, we had several people who were extras in it. Like my middle school principal was in one of the court scenes.

Honestly, I was very excited about the experience itself. But afterwards, I didn't have a desire to do any more acting. It was kind of intimidating: the whole getting your lines right and having to do that over and over again, and coming in at the exact right time to say something. It was fun and exciting to meet everyone, but it was kind of also a funny experience where you try to maneuver your way around something that you've never done before.

You were only twelve.

Yeah, I was only twelve.

There were some funny things that had to happen beforehand. I had very dark-toned skin. I had to go to school at the end of the school year and wear sun block, hats, and long-sleeves—and we're in Charleston, South Carolina. I mean, it was hot! I had to make sure I didn't get tan at all, because that lighter skin was what everybody was supposed to have. The wealthier families, I guess, were more indoors. My mother had to send me to school every day, [it was] sweltering at recess, and I'm covered in sun block and hats and long sleeves so that I didn't get a tan.

That sounds like a little bit of an ordeal.

Yeah, it was interesting—that part of it, I do remember.

Everybody around was really supportive about it. They were all excited. They wanted to know things. The first thing everybody asked was, "Did you meet Patrick Swayze?" "Yes, I did. I had a scene with him." They'd ask me my lines. It was a fun experience.

Sometimes, I'm in my normal, everyday life and I completely forget about it. And years down the road, I'll be talking to a friend, and somehow the subject comes up and they don't know that had ever happened. It's something that is exciting and fun to talk about it, but you don't just bring it up in every conversation. You go along and somebody says, "I had no idea you were in that movie!"

The *North and South*—A Novel for Television Facebook group has so many people in it.

It's overwhelming. It's exciting. When I joined [the Facebook group], I started throwing some pictures up in there and I got a lot of questions, one after the other. It got to a point where it was a little overwhelming. I'm just the average gal. I'm not even famous. I can't imagine somebody who is actually in movies all the time.

Look at Patrick—how famous he got.

I know. It's amazing.

It was a big deal for our town, too. They started doing things to the houses there, and covering the roads, and just blocking off areas where they filmed. That was a huge deal in Charleston at the time because South Carolina was known, but it wasn't like now—how it's kind of a go-to-vacation spot for people and a lot of people have moved there. But at the time, it was smaller. So it was a big deal for our little town to have that happening. Everybody was excited and going there to watch and trying to show up and see what they could see at the downtown set area.

You certainly have a lot of good memories.

Yeah, I do. It was an experience, like I said. My mom and I, [we had] one of those things for us to bond together. I really enjoyed it.

Sue Tabashnik

SCOTT WILDER

Stuntman: *Point Break*, *Black Dog*, and *The Renegades*

*Email and Telephone Interviews: January 2017 and July 2023
Written By Scott Wilder*

My father, Glenn Wilder, was the second unit director and stunt coordinator on *Point Break*. He really loved and appreciated Patrick's abilities and "go for it" attitude.

Patrick's character in *Point Break* had to surf, skydive, and do extensive car and foot chases. His brother, Don, was a master skydiver. Patrick would take off after the work day ended and head to the Santa Monica airport and fly to Perris to do a jump or two with his brother and other instructors. Patrick couldn't wait to "fly"—he danced like a bird in the air! He was stoked to tell us about it the next day at work and was always hoping to get off work early to go for a jump.

Early in the production, some of the surfing stuntmen and me took Patrick to Little Dume to surf. One early morning, we went hiking down to the beach. While we were talking about his skydiving from the night before, he slipped and slid down the ravine, laughing the whole way. He climbed out and we went for a surf. After surfing, we were jamming back to the car and went to [the] set. When he went into his trailer, he realized he had lost his watch, the gold Rolex his father had given him. We had a busy couple of weeks working from call to wrap. When we got a chance a few weeks later, we went to surf, and Patrick gleefully saw the watch in the spot in the ravine where he had been. It was like Christmas to him! It blew his mind.

One day, Patrick and Keanu [Reeves] were shooting a scene in which they were playing aggressive football and there was a tackle into the water. Patrick felt something pop in his knee. He was willing to do another take, but they had gotten the shot. The following day, I went to say hello and his doctor was draining the fluid from his knee with a giant syringe. When I walked in with surprise on my face, he looked up and smiled and said,

"Hey, how was *your* night?"

I had to double Patrick on the foot chase because he was out promoting *Ghost* for two weeks in Europe. Due to the Ronald Reagan mask [his character wore], I was able to do most of the chase.

I worked with Patrick early in his career on the TV series *The Renegades* [1983]. The final time I worked with him was after *Point Break,* on the movie *Black Dog.*

Patrick always made time to tell us stories. From the first day on *The Renegades* until the last day on *Black Dog,* he was always kind and sweet and treated all of the stuntmen and myself like brothers.

TOM SANDERS

Stunt Skydiving Cameraman, *Point Break*

Written by Tom Sanders April 30, 2017, Updated March 13, 2023

It is a BIG deal that Patrick trained and became a proficient skydiver to do some of the actual stunts involving skydiving. This is unheard of in Hollywood. I have been a SAG stunt skydiving cameraman for nearly forty years and he and Tom Cruise (Tom in recent history) are the only ones I recall doing their own stunts. They all say they do, but they don't. Patrick was a skydiver. He was the REAL DEAL in all aspects of life.

Regarding Patrick during the filming of *Point Break* over Perris Valley Drop Zone, Patrick called me up one day after the studio thought they had everything they needed. He asked me if I would come out to Perris. He would bring the 35mm movie film, if I could bring the camera and make some jumps. Since this location did not match Lake Powell or California City where the two scenes were shot, I concentrated on up-angle exit shots, track bys and deployments, but had to get one shot with the Perris scenery during the day. We didn't get paid. Who would care? He just wanted, like me, to make the scenes as good as possible.

Sue Tabashnik

RAY COTTINGHAM
Stunt Skydiving Cameraman, *Point Break*

Written by Ray Cottingham: March 16, 2023

I am sure Tom Sanders gave you the background on the *Point Break* aerial filming. Post-production, Patrick was able and wanted to do some of his own jump sequences. We filmed for several days at California City Drop Zone and Perris Valley Drop Zone. At Perris Valley, I shot some 35mm still film of Tom Sanders, Kevin Donnelly, and Patrick, and of Patrick doing freestyle or aerial, dance-type poses for him. He had less than fifty jumps and amazed me with his relaxed and natural skill. Since I was also shooting 35mm cine, I had to attempt up-angle shots, because the original jump was filmed over Lake Powell.

    I was impressed with Patrick's overall friendly and relaxed manner. Only one other time in years of filming aerial stunts have I relaxed with a major movie star—Paul Hogan, in 1974, while filming a commercial in Australia. I have some 35mm still photos of the above jumps at Perris Valley.

PATRICK YOUNGBLOOD

Talks About Frances and Sam Youngblood, Extras, *North and South*

Telephone Interview: July 14, 2023

I think you wrote me that your aunt and uncle were on the set of *North and South* Book One?

Yes. So basically the context is, my aunt, Frances Youngblood, and uncle, Sam Youngblood, lived in Charleston. They were both on my dad's side of the family, and they have both passed away.

I'm sorry.

It's been a while. My dad was a lot older. I was born in '73 and he was born in '25. So that's why they both passed on; they were just both up there in age. They were professional extras because Charleston got a lot of work. It still kind of does—not what it used to get in the eighties and nineties, though. My uncle had done one movie I think, in 1983. They got to know a local casting director there named Lorraine Maxwell Young. She was in Summerville, South Carolina. When *North and South* came along, Sam got cast as President Buchanan. This was probably 1985, so I was still quite young. (Lorraine got my uncle a lot of work—my aunt didn't want that much. The last notable thing they did was *The Notebook,* 2005.)

They told us stories about everything that happened. My aunt had developed a really good relationship with the casting director, who gave her a car pass to get out on to properties, like Boone Hall. The plantations that they filmed on were closed to the public due to filming. She also would wander around downtown Charleston whenever they were over at Boone Hall.

Sam got [cast] in Book One. His scene was with Hal Holbrook and Rachel Jakes, who was John Jakes' wife. She played Mary Todd Lincoln in this scene. She didn't have any speaking parts, and neither did my uncle.

The other people involved in this scene were Morgan Fairchild, Philip Casnoff, Genie Francis, and John Stockwell.

My uncle was basically sitting out there in the carriage waiting for Lincoln and Mrs. Lincoln to come out. Hal Holbrook was Lincoln. He helps Mrs. Lincoln into the carriage. Hal Holbrook turns and waves to the people, and he gets in the carriage, and the carriage goes off.

Before the thing came out, we had seen a picture in the newspaper of this particular scene which was a really good shot. Certainly, that's not it. There's got to be more Sam than this. None of his scenes involved Patrick Swayze.

With Frances having the car pass, she went out to Boone Hall—which was Mount Royal in the miniseries—almost every day. She went so often, that at the end of Book One, the director, David L. Wolper—gave her a certificate from the cast and crew for being the most important fan, or something like that, the biggest fan. It was something cute. They also gave her Patrick Swayze's nameplate that was on his trailer because they were done at the end of Book One. Back in the eighties, I guess it was safer then. They just put the actor's name on the trailer (rather than the character's name). They gave her his nameplate because they were done with Book One. They were taking their break, which I believe was like two or three months in between Book One and Book Two.

My aunt obviously took a lot of pictures on set. She got autographs, because back then there were no phones to do selfies. She got Patrick's autograph. She got to see him on a regular basis. She said he was really nice.

This [TV miniseries] was really the thing that I think got him going in the US. I heard on a documentary that *North and South* put Patrick on the map in the US, and then when he did *Dirty Dancing*, he was on the map internationally. My aunt said he was wonderful, very nice. She said most of the cast was. It was a day-to-day experience of seeing him. She got to know most of the cast and crew—those who were willing to talk. There was nothing negative spoken about Patrick that I had ever heard. She came across as a very grandmotherly type because like I said, she was retired. She had to have talked to Patrick on a regular basis. I remember who she said was friendly on set and who wasn't. The majority of the cast was very nice.

She said it was very entertaining to watch. That's pretty much the long and the short of it. I have heard stories about other cast members, and you have to wonder if they were that way because they were method acting.

Of course, when Book Two came around, my aunt went back and watched some more. They weren't in town as much for that as they were for Book One. Then Book Three came around years later, and that was a whole different program.

Your aunt sounds so fabulous.

She was. She was funny and also amusing. So they probably felt the same way. I just remember hearing these stories, and I was listening on the edge of my seat, and I hadn't even seen the show yet. I didn't even know what these people looked like, for the most part. You know, when she told me like Morgan Fairchild and Elizabeth Taylor, those people I knew. But Patrick Swayze and James Read and Terri Garber and Kirstie Alley, I did not know.

Right. So many of those people have passed on.

Yes. Kirstie, most recently.

Wow, this is really interesting.

When I started this [Facebook] group [in 2017] that you saw me in, I did that prior to the *North and South* Hollywood Show [2018]. Are you familiar with the Hollywood Show?

I am not.

It is basically a meet-and-greet convention, so it's kind of like a comic-con, but it's for television-oriented work, shows of the past: like *Dynasty*, *Knots Landing*. I believe *North and South* was done in 2018. It consisted of James Read and his wife, Wendy Kilbourne—whom he had met while filming *North and South* and married. Morgan Fairchild was there, and Mitch Ryan, Terri Garber, Lesley-Anne Down, Philip Casnoff, Lewis Smith, and William Ostrander. There's one I am forgetting.

In the last few months, it [the Facebook group] has taken off; it went from 3,000 to 5,000 people very quickly, and it's about to hit 10,000. Like, oh my gosh! [On October 11, 2024, this Facebook group has 26.7K members.] There is a fan base, and it's very international. A lot of people from Germany love the series. One of them commented on a post that up until a few of years ago, they were showing *North and South* on Christmas every year.

Unfortunately, I didn't get the chance to be in either one of those [Book One and Book Two]. Subsequently, a year after Book Two came out, I went up there and I was an extra in a couple of movies. But I wish I would have had the opportunity to do either one of those, even though those summer months would have been just torture.

Yeah. I can't imagine wearing those costumes in the heat.

There's the heat and the bugs—in the Deep South in the low country in South Carolina.

Somebody posted a picture the other day of the actors on a break. It's Genie Francis, Terri Garber, and I think one other person in the photo. They're just sitting in the shade, and they had fans, the kind that you wave in front of your face. Genie just really looks miserable. I understand. I wouldn't have a smile on my face either, if that was my situation.

I was reading somewhere that Patrick passed out or maybe almost passed out from the heat several times, but I am not sure if that was *North and South* or a different movie. [I remember Patrick talking about it.]

It could have been *North and South*. He had a cold at one point. I believe it was in Book One. I don't see how some of the women didn't literally have fainting spells. Everything covered from head to toe. It was the real deal. I mean the boots, all the layers, and the wigs.

Yes. I did read in a lot of places that Patrick really loved playing his role of Orry.

He has a couple of chapters about *North and South* in his memoir (but they were cut out of the audiobook).

PATRICK SWAYZE Still Inspiring!

AMY OSBORN
Extra (Uncredited), *The Outsiders*

JOE CERVANTEZ
Extra (Credited), *The Outsiders*

Telephone Interview with Amy and Joe: June 30, 2024

*Both Amy and Joe work at The Outsiders House Museum in Tulsa, Oklahoma which is the home that was used for shooting the movie. The museum showcases memorabilia and photos, and offers tours.

Amy: The only thing that I did with Patrick or talked to him at all or anything like that—was just for one moment on the set. I walked by and he had a football. I actually kind of threw my arms up thinking maybe he'll throw me the ball and he did. I turned around and threw it to somebody else and then they threw it back to me, and then I threw it to somebody else, and they threw it back to me. That was pretty much the extent of me having anything to do with Patrick out on the set. Now Joe didn't really talk to him out on the set much, but he did talk to him at the premiere.

Amy, how did you happen to be on the set?

Amy: I was thirteen years old on the set. I was with my best friend and her mom. Her mom actually had a 1957 Chevy Nomad that was pre-approved to be out at the Admiral Twin Drive-in, driving it around, just trying to get it in the movie. It never did make it in the movie.

Oh, sorry.

Amy: That's the way I was out there. The way I got in the movie was, I just got out of the car and walked through the scene and they had to cut. They asked if I wanted to be in the movie and sent me down to wardrobe.

Are you serious? So you ended up being an extra?

Amy: Yes, I was an unpaid extra—an accidental extra, if you will. I would just be considered an uncredited, background extra.

Now you're working at the museum. What do you do there?

Amy: I can do pretty much everything. I do private tours and private screenings. I tour people when they come in the house in open hours. I am in charge of doing the school tours that come through the house. As well as, like, if we have a leak or whatever happens at the house, I am the one who usually tells the bosses and then they get it done.

So this movie really connected with you?

Amy: Yes, absolutely. You know, just growing up on basically the wrong side of the tracks. I was adopted—always kind of felt like an outsider. I actually didn't read the book until we finished filming. Then I told my mom, "Would you buy me the book *The Outsiders*?" I was not a reader. She was like, "Who are you and what have you done with my daughter?" I loved the book and probably read it maybe only three or four times until audiobooks. I have listened to it several times on audiobook.

That was pretty much the extent of me getting in the movie and coming up here. I've been here almost three years now.

Oh, wow.

So Patrick was throwing a football around because they were in between takes?

Amy: Here's the story on that. Basically, Patrick Swayze, Emilio Estevez, C. Thomas Howell, and Darren Dalton were all standing outside of the makeup trailers. They had just got their makeup put on. So that means the rest of the cast members were in there getting their makeup put on while those four were already finished. Patrick was just holding a football. Me and my best friend at the time, we wanted to get on the football team at our school. Of course, they wouldn't let us even try out. So anybody ever holding a football, I'm going to run and try to get them to throw it to me. And that's exactly what happened with Patrick.

I did not know who he was. I knew he was going to be in the movie, simply because they had just got their makeup put on and they were in their complete outfits ready to go out and do a photo shoot. Literally, I just kind of jogged a little and threw up my arms like I was going to catch a football. He literally bombed me that ball and I started running like I was in the NFL.

That's a great story! He was almost going to be a professional football player, but he injured his [left] knee playing football as a high school senior.

Amy: I didn't know that, so that's an even cooler story.

So Joe, you were at the premiere for *The Outsiders*?

Joe: Yes, I was at the premiere, and just to start a conversation with Patrick—I already knew the answer, but I asked him, "Who did the handstand on the fence rail in front of the house?" And he told me it was him. I told him, "Well, I have a picture of it." So he proceeds to get his wallet out and give me a business card that said "Buddy Swayze, carpenter." I saw the documentary *I Am Patrick Swayze,* and I found out that whenever he and his wife moved from New York to California, they didn't have any money coming in, so they did carpentry work.

That's right.

Joe: So he had this business card and he took one out of his wallet. He wrote his phone number on the back of the card and gave it to me.

I called him the next week after the premiere. I told him the pictures I sell are twenty dollars each. I told him I would sell him that picture for twenty-five dollars and mail it to him (the extra five dollars being for the mailer and postage), but he didn't want to buy it. He said he would get one from the studio photographer. He hadn't made *Dirty Dancing* or *Ghost* yet. So I figured he wasn't rolling in money.

That's right.

Joe: He may have used his money to buy his ranch. I don't know when he bought his ranch [1984—after being cast in *North and South*]. This was in 1983.

That's pretty cool to be at the premiere of *The Outsiders*.

Joe: Yeah.

So anyway, that was pretty much my interaction with Patrick.

I did take some other pictures of him in the makeup trailer. I would walk into the makeup trailer like I owned the place and just walk over to whoever was sitting in the makeup chair. I've got a picture of Patrick—at least two pictures of him in the makeup chair.

One picture I have of him, I was shooting into a mirror—that's the only way I could get a picture of him in the makeup chair. One picture you can see me in the mirror off to the left side taking the picture. I call that the first selfie.

That's cute.

Joe: And he's lighting up a cigarette at the makeup table. Then I've got a close-up of him and it looks like the makeup artist maybe is working on his eyebrows. And I've got a really good, nice close-up of him being made up by the makeup artist.

So I have two pictures in the makeup trailer, plus the picture of him doing the handstand on the fence rail.

Oh, wow! I'm just wondering, I've seen a photo on Facebook of Patrick getting made up. Who knows, there's probably a lot of photos going around. I wonder if that's your photo?

Joe: I don't know. In the close-up picture, you can see the shoulder of the makeup artist on the right side of the picture. I couldn't tell the makeup artist to get out of the way. If I had told him that, I would have been escorted out of the trailer.

Yeah, I'm surprised you got in there in the first place.

Joe: Yeah. But that picture is a really good close-up of Patrick; a really nice, good focus, and everything.

So it sounds like you had a really great experience with Patrick.

Joe: Yeah. He was very nice, very down-to-earth, a really likable person. I really liked him, especially after I saw the documentary *I Am Patrick Swayze*. I really liked that documentary. I think I have the movie *One Last Dance*.

I was at the premiere of *One Last Dance* [2003] in Houston. A bunch of us fans went there. I thought the dancing in the movie was really exquisite. Did you like it?

Joe: Yeah, I did.

Amy: Yeah, I did, too.

Joe: I really thought a lot of Patrick. I thought he was just a really cool guy. I didn't really talk to him during the production of the movie. I saw him from a distance.

So you were a paid extra?

Joe: Yes. Do you remember the scene where the two guys pull out knives and they're scuffling?

Sort of. It's been a minute since I watched it, to be honest. Are you one of those guys?

Joe: No, I'm not one of the guys fighting, but I'm one of the crowd. You can pick me out because I'm the only baldheaded one in there. I was thirty-eight years old and I turned thirty-nine that summer on July 3rd, which is also Tom Cruise's birthday. I didn't find out until later on that Tom Cruise and I share the same birthday. Tom turned sixty-one last year on July 3rd [2023] and I turned eighty.

Congratulations. That's a milestone.
   So you also work at the museum?

Joe: Yes. I'm here on the weekends. I'm here selling the photos. I have a large collection of photos that I took during the filming of *The Outsiders,* so I sell those here at the museum.

You have fans from all over the world visit the museum?

Joe: We have fans from all over the US, plus foreign countries.

What kind of memorabilia in the museum do you have of Patrick?

Amy: I honestly think that the only memorabilia is the pictures that Joe took and we do have one yearbook that has his picture in there twice. Of course, we have Joe's business card that Patrick gave to him.

Anything else you can think of about Patrick?

Amy: I did take a picture of Patrick myself. When they told me his name, he was so unknown still at the time, I heard Patrick Swain, so that's what's on the back of my Polaroid picture. Emilio Estevez was in the same picture and of course I wrote down his name was Milo Estrada: literally, totally unknown to me at the age of thirteen. Of course, Patrick had something that came out before *The Outsiders*, when I was younger.

Skatetown U.S.A. [1979] and I guess *North and South* was later—1985—after *The Outsiders*.

Amy: *Skatetown U.S.A.*, yeah. I did see the skate scene of him whipping that thing [belt] around. He was just such a handsome guy.

Yeah. He got really good reviews. Then he was offered a three-picture deal, but he didn't want to be in the movies just because he was good-looking [so he didn't take the deal]. He wanted to take the craft seriously.

Amy: That's right.
Joe: I bought the *North and South* series a while back. I know it was on TV, but I didn't watch all of it. So I went and bought the whole series. I like Civil War history. I bought it because Patrick is in it.

MICHAEL PORTERFIELD
Mountain Lake Hotel Lead Line Cook, *Dirty Dancing*

Here are two anecdotes from my March 2009 interview of Michael Porterfield from the book *The Fans' Love Story: How the Movie* DIRTY DANCING *Captured the Hearts of Millions!* (2010) by Sue Tabashnik. Michael worked as the lead line cook during the shooting of *Dirty Dancing* at Mountain Lake Hotel in Virginia. He recently retired from his position as executive chef there. Michael and his family have a very strong connection to Mountain Lake as his family owned it in the late 1880s.

FIRST STORY
I'll tell you about Buddy. He came in the kitchen one night to get his beers. We had a dishwasher who had just recently gotten out of the Marines. This was a really weird little guy. The only way we could get him to work was to let him drink wine. He brought his own wine. We didn't provide it. We let

him drink it 'cause he would stay there and work. It was Maddog or Red Lady 21—one of those fortified wines. Buddy came back in there and was talking with him. Buddy asked him, "Do you want a drink of beer?" and he said, "Sure," and he [the dishwasher] had a big pull on the bottle. We just got a big kick out of that. Buddy was a really down-to-earth guy. He was not in the least bit pretentious. He would invite us out to the library to have beers with him.

SECOND STORY

It was late one evening and we were done with dinner, and we had cleaned up and were getting ready to leave. They had a crew that did nothing but drive from Blacksburg to Mountain Lake. It was a lucrative job to have. They paid ten dollars an hour. That was very good pay then to just drive people back and forth. They stopped that around seven o'clock in the evening and Buddy needed a ride to Blacksburg and came through and asked several people. Most of them rode together and were way up on the other end of the county.

So Buddy got to the back dock, and I was up there, and he said, "Can you give me a ride?"

I said, "Yep, can you ride on a motorcycle?"

"Oh, that's no problem."

He had the black leather jacket on. He was ready. I had an extra helmet, much to the chagrin of my cousin, who also had a motorcycle but didn't have an extra helmet.

So we loaded up on the bike and headed down the mountain. Now you've driven up the mountain; you know how curvy it is. When we got on the bike, he was holding on. It has a metal strap on the back and he was holding on to that. We started down the mountain and about on the third curve, he grabbed me . . . and that's how he held on until we got to Blacksburg. When we got there, he was joking, and we were laughing.

Sue Tabashnik

MIKE HAMMOND

Patrick's Security at Whitehall and Tremont Hotels in Chicago, *Next of Kin*

Telephone Interview: May 8, 2024

Could you please talk about how you met Patrick?

Sure. I graduated from Indiana State University with a criminology degree in August of 1987. I grew up in Indiana, but I spent a lot of time in Chicago—I had an aunt here, and my grandmother lived up here for a long time, and my dad for a short time.

There's an Irish family in Chicago called Moran. My family was close with their family. Three of the five sons were policemen, one was a fireman and the other worked for the city.

Wow!

Yeah, very typical Chicago Irish-Catholic family. One of them, Barry Moran, second-to-the-oldest, was kind of a legendary detective in the Chicago Police Department. When I graduated from college, he had a side-job as director of security at the Whitehall and Tremont Hotels, which are kind of back-to-back. One is on Chestnut Street and one is on Delaware Street, right off Michigan Avenue. They're kind of small, European-style, luxury hotels. They operated as one community, back then. They were owned by the same guy. I don't know if they still are. They're still active. They're still very nice.

He offered me a job working for him, back then we were called "house detectives"—security for the hotels. We wore a coat and tie and kind of roamed the property. We had a lot of stars, musicians, rock stars who stayed with us because they liked that the Whitehall and Tremont were more service-driven, smaller hotels. I took that job in the spring of 1988.

Sometime later in that year, Patrick was in town. They were filming parts of the movie *Next of Kin* here in Chicago. The movie was largely based in Chicago [some filming was also done in Kentucky]. Patrick stayed with us for two to three months while they were filming that movie. There were a lot people in it who later became big stars, including Billy Paxton and Liam Neeson. Patrick was far and away the biggest star. *Dirty Dancing* had already come out.

He stayed in one of our big suites, which was like a two-bedroom apartment. It was really big. He had his two dogs. I don't remember what breed they were, but they were like greyhound-size, long-haired dogs. Are you familiar?

I know that his dog he was very close with was named Cody, but I'm not sure if that was one of the dogs.

There is no way I could remember that.

Right.

He had a habit of going out and walking the dogs late at night, past midnight to two a.m. I worked ten p.m. to six a.m. Barry called Patrick "The Kid." When we figured this out, he told me, "Mike, any time 'The Kid' walks those dogs, I want you with him." At first, Patrick was a little resistant because he was kind of a tough guy. He wasn't that big. I don't know his height and weight, but I'm guessing maybe 5'7, 5'8, maybe 150 pounds. He was lean and muscular. He thought of himself as kind of a tough guy. He was a martial artist. He was in great shape. But, you know, it wasn't about that for us. We didn't want anything to happen to the big movie star while he's staying at our hotel.

He was never a jerk about it. He's just like, "You don't need to be walking with me." I said, "I kind of do because my boss told me I had to." After that one time, he was really good to me, very nice. We had some fun conversations and that became a regular thing. We let him keep his Harley-Davidson in our security office in the Whitehall Hotel. He would also go out at night and ride his motorcycle. He wouldn't wear a helmet, which we gave him grief about. A funny thing, I would remember for whatever reason, he would put tape over his ear drums, I guess so the wind didn't bother his ears.

So that's how I met him and got to know him.

It seems like after that first time, things went well.

Yeah, it really did. I think it went well because I rarely asked him anything about being a movie star or an actor or anything like that. I was pretty young myself. I would have been twenty-three. I had the wherewithal or was shy enough that I wasn't starstruck.

One of the few conversations (when I asked) him about being a star or being an actor, I asked, "Who are some of the people you really like or people you didn't like?" He said, "It wouldn't be right to talk about people I didn't like. I wouldn't want that done to me." He said, "Most of the people I have worked with I liked." He did mention some people he liked a lot were Sam Elliott and Jeff Bridges. He just said, "They're two really good guys, down-to-earth."

Sam Elliott has always talked very highly of Patrick [as far as I know]. So did Liam Neeson. In an *ABC News* interview by Mara Reinstein that aired on April 13, 2022 titled "SUPERSTAR Patrick Swayze," Liam talked about Patrick. He spoke about how Patrick gave him some tips on how to do fight scenes, and how he appreciated that Patrick was teaching him and looking out for him because he was new to the US.

They told me Liam Neeson was a really good boxer when he was growing up in Ireland. I can kind of picture in my head that conversation taking place.

Did Liam Neeson stay in the hotel?

I just don't recall. I know for sure that I saw Billy Paxton. I am pretty sure Paxton stayed at the hotel because I knew who he was. He wasn't super-well known at the time. He had been in *Weird Science* [1985] and *Streets of Fire* [1984], which is a movie I really liked a lot.

Patrick, I really got to know more because Barry had assigned me to walk with him when he went out. I didn't have interaction with other movie stars and famous people because they weren't there as long as Patrick.

The only other time I had that much interaction was with Whitney Houston, and that was only over about a forty-eight-hour period. She was in town promoting her album with the song "I Wanna Dance with Somebody (Who Loves Me)." She was awesome, very sweet, and beautiful.

That's so tragic about her.

It really was. It was painful. I only knew her for a short time, but it was painful the way she ended.

I had read that to prep for his role in *Next of Kin*, Patrick rode with real police officers and initially they gave him a hard time, but I guess it all turned out okay. Do you have any info on that?

I do recall that he had done a ride-along with the police department, but I don't recall the details of it. I think I told you I was trying to find this article, probably in the *Chicago Sun-Times*, about when Patrick was filming somewhere in the city and he saw a purse snatcher grab a woman's purse. He chased the guy down and got the purse back. We only knew about it because it was in the paper. I was trying to find it. It was probably in either Michael Sneed's column or in Irv Kupcinet's column in the *Chicago Sun-Times*.

Wow! I have another question. I would be totally remiss if I did not ask, since you are retired law enforcement. Did you happen to see any of Patrick's TV show *The Beast* in which he played an FBI agent, sort of on the edge?

I did not see it. I heard of it. I told you, I was kicking myself a little bit because when I heard he was sick, I really felt like I should have reached out to him, because my mother had passed away from pancreatic cancer.

I am so sorry.

Thank you.

As kind of off-hand as that sounds—Oh, you can reach out and talk to a movie star—I feel like as a homicide detective, I probably could have gotten him on the phone had I tried hard enough. Then it really hurt me when I realized that he had been here in Chicago filming that show *The Beast*. I may have watched an episode just to see him, but I don't really recall it too much. At that time, I was just too busy.

Do you have a favorite movie that Patrick did?

Probably *The Outsiders*. I really liked him in that as the big brother. There are none of his movies that I don't like. I mean, I don't think *Next of Kin* is a good movie, but I liked seeing him in it. *Road House* is so campy.

Yeah. I tell you what, in my opinion, his *Road House* is a lot better than the new one.

Yeah, for sure. I mean, it's really tough sledding to try and beat Patrick Swayze in anything. That's also a fun film.

Ghost is probably his best film. Actually, I think *The Outsiders* is really underrated, for him especially, one of the great roles. It was really, really a great movie. He was the biggest star in that movie. Once again, Matt Dillon, Tom Cruise, Rob Lowe—there were a lot of people in it who would become big stars.

Patrick and Rob Lowe were in that hockey movie, *Youngblood* [1986].

Right.

It's worth watching Joe Rogan interview Rob Lowe because he talks about Patrick a little bit [Episode #1522 of "The Joe Rogan Experience," air date August 7, 2022]. When I first saw it, I thought Rob was kind of making fun of Patrick. I watched it again. He's not, really. He's just talking about Patrick's intensity. He was an intense guy. He was very disciplined in his fitness routine. He walked fast. He walked with purpose. I rewatched that interview, and now I think it is pretty cute and funny. I can imagine that was what it was like to work with Patrick. Especially, Rob was very young when they did *The Outsiders*.

What was he like sixteen or something? [He was seventeen and turned eighteen during the filming of the movie.]

I liked *Youngblood* and Patrick again was very good. I think that was Keanu Reeves' first film.

That's right. He was in there.

He was the goalie. It's funny that Rob Lowe told Joe Rogan that he didn't know for most of the film that Keanu Reeves was an actor. He thought he was an actual Canadian hockey goalie.

That is funny.

Those kinds of really physical roles served Patrick well because that's the way he was. He was in great shape and he carried himself with a very physical intensity.

So did Patrick work out at the hotel?

No, we didn't have work-out facilities there. It was a small, European-like hotel.

He talked about working out all of the time.

I guess he got a pretty good workout when he was working around his ranch.

Yeah, it seems like it. The documentaries I've seen show him as a true horseman, just a very physical guy.

Nowadays, I think everybody accepts dancers are in great shape.

I think, in retrospect, dancing to Patrick was a fitness routine. It was part of his fitness because his mother was a dance instructor.

We talked a lot about martial arts because I was a wrestler, a judo guy. I remember talking about him being into karate and kick-boxing, a little bit.

Wow! So interesting. It's so cool that you had time with Patrick.

Now, especially, I cherish that time with him. I think part of the reason he was so open with me: one, it occurs to me that he's just a really good human being. Also, I think because I was just a kid and I was naïve and I wasn't starstruck at all. He was kind of more open to me. When he left, he gave me a bunch of his dailies.

What?

You know, like his daily schedule and stuff. He was just like, "I'm going to toss this. Do you want it?" I'm like, "Sure!" I mean, 'cause it's Patrick Swayze. I've met so many famous people throughout the years and with the exception of Bobby Knight, I have very few pictures or autographs. I never asked for them. That was before cell phones. Even when they came around or even now, it's just not my style.

Do you still have the dailies?

No, I do not personally have them because I gave them all to my mom.

That's sweet.

She was the opposite of me, she was super-starstruck. Anytime, anybody famous, I made sure to tell my mom because she just thought it was the coolest thing in the world.

When my mom passed away, we found the dailies in her nightstand. I think my brother Andrew probably has the dailies. If we find that stuff, we should probably donate them.

Absolutely.

I have a lot of affection for that memory of that time with him. That first year for me in Chicago—Patrick is a highlight.

Did you see the Barbara Walters interview [the second one—2009]?

I did—that was painful, painful.

Afterwards, he said maybe he shouldn't have done it.

Good-looking movie star—I think that tells you the measure of a man, because that was totally putting aside his ego. He did it totally without ego, just to be a voice for people suffering like that. I think you're right, by any definition, he was a hero.

How long were you a police officer?

Twenty-two years a police officer. I was a detective for the last sixteen of those years.

GLENN WATKINS

Reenactor, *North and South*

Telephone Interview: October 12, 2023

You were a reenactor in *North and South*. Could you please explain what a reenactor is?

We are people who are interested in history. We go out and recreate Civil War battles and reenactments and also living histories at national parks and certain events. We basically recreate the life of the common soldier: camping, tents, drills, marching, battles. We specialize in authenticity. So we have all of the maneuvers down. That's why movie companies like to hire us, because all they have to do is say, "Start." They don't have to direct us on how to do all that. We were telling them, "That didn't look right" or "This is the way it's supposed to look."

We didn't get paid as extras. We got paid extra money because of our expertise. Plus, we provide uniforms, equipment, material, cannons, and horses, all of it.

That sounds amazing. Are there a lot of reenactor groups that do this?

In past times, there were a lot of us. We had 20-30,000 of us across the country who would come together and do full-scale reenactments, and a lot of smaller, local ones. Over the years, the passion has died down a little bit. We still have some, but they're not on the scale of the eighties and nineties.

Are you still doing it?

No, I quit doing it a while back. I'm just getting too old. I did it for thirty-five to forty years.

Well, thirty-five to forty years is a long time. Were you in *North and South* Books One and Two?

Just Book Two.

Did you have any interactions with Patrick Swayze?

I had three or four interactions with him personally. They were pretty interesting.

What happened during those interactions?

The first time we met him, we had our camps set up out there—rows and rows of tents. Our tent was next to the end. There were four of us staying there. We had our big tent set up and a big fire going out front. Normally, when we set up camps, we set them up to be authentic. We camp and live like how the soldiers lived in the 1860s. But since we were going to be there three-and-a half weeks, we made it more modern on the inside. We had a TV with rabbit ears on it. We had cots, coolers, lanterns. We were grilling steaks and baked potatoes out on our fire.

Patrick and two other people were walking back through the camp. He said, "You all are living high on the hog!" He saw inside our tent, "You have more stuff here than I have in my room." None of us lived in hotel rooms. We lived on the set, so we wanted to make it as comfortable as possible. We invited him to have a steak, but he said he was headed out. He was impressed with our ability to cope with the filming situation. That was the first time I met him.

Another time, we were rehearsing a scene where, out in the field, you could see just a mass of Yankee soldiers forming to attack. They were rehearsing the scene. A courier came up to Patrick (General Main) and handed him a note that said the Yankees were going to attack. So he picked up his binoculars and looked out over the field and said, "Holy shit! Let's get the f… out of here!" Everybody just died laughing. He was really a jokester, but he could snap right back into his part easily, quite professionally.

I fondly remember him. He was easy to work with. He made it pleasurable. A lot of stress can be in these scenes because you want to rehearse them right. You can't just keep re-taking and re-taking them, because of all the background stuff going on: all of the fire techniques, all of the stunt work going on. It takes a lot of coordination and focus. You have to focus a lot to make sure you're doing it right. So to break the tension, he was really cordial and a lot of fun to be around.

I've been in seventeen other movie productions. I was in *Glory;* I got to work with Matthew Broderick, Denzel Washington, and Morgan Freeman. I was in a bunch of Ted Turner productions: *Gettysburg, Gods and Generals,* and *Andersonville.* In *Andersonville,* I had a speaking part—I was a Confederate sergeant. A lot of these films, we'd film in the morning as the Yankees and be behind the fence shooting. We'd go eat lunch and then change into Confederate uniforms and would be running across the field to get the Yankees. I have two movies where you can see me actually killing myself. We'd take a hundred guys and make it look like ten thousand guys. Toward the end of my movies, we started doing some weird movies. We did *Abraham Lincoln: Vampire Hunter.* After that, I did *The Vampire Diaries;* they had a civil war. That was my last movie—about eight, nine, ten years ago. I just turned seventy.

It was no different than my music business because that's what I do for a living. I'm a musician. I play fifteen instruments. I've played with Willie Nelson, Hank Williams, Jr., Neil Young, Travis Tritt.

You played guitar or drums?

I played bass and was a back-up singer. I lived on tour buses forever. It's just large productions—concerts, shows. You have to be a good musician to do those jobs, but the name of the job really is to make the star look good. It's the same thing as the reenactor job.

You mentioned that you made the tent modern on the set of *North and South*, but I'm sure it was really hot.

Actually, it was in the fall and it was pretty comfortable. You learned how to live like the soldiers did. . . . I was a living historian. I was a volunteer in the National Guard Service. I was bonded to be able to shoot a musket. I was an official shooter on a lot of these sets. I was in the Marines for three years during Viet Nam. I'm an expert with weapons, so that's right down my alley.

Oh, wow! Three years!
So it sounds like in *North and South*, Patrick was prepared and knew what he was doing.

Oh, yeah. As many movies as I worked with and as many big stars I worked with, I got to see a comparison of different actors and how they approached their craft. To see him hanging out with us, you would think he doesn't know what he's doing, because he's having too much fun with us. But he could snap right back into his character so fast and be dead serious. He was depending on us to make him look good. We were professionals, and he was super-professional. He liked hanging out with us because he saw how seriously we took our hobby. He was very serious, hard-working, and well-rehearsed. He enjoyed working with us and we enjoyed working with him. He appreciated that we put out a hundred percent.

He was one of the first big stars that I worked with because that was one of the first movies I did, so I learned a lot.

A lot of memories!

Working with him was definitely a stand-out. It helped build a foundation for learning how to work in the movie business.

He was a good athlete, too. He's done quite a few scenes where he was very athletic. What was that movie he did with the bar scenes?

Road House?

Yeah, *Road House*. People see that on film, but they don't realize how hard that is to pull off those kind of fight scenes. And you have to be very athletic and in good shape to do it.

How many reenactors were there on the *North and South* set?

On some days, there were maybe a couple hundred of us, and on other days there was a couple thousand, depending on the scene that they were shooting. There was a basic core unit of us. We would change uniforms—we'd be Confederates, and then we'd be Yankees, and then we'd switch it up.

I saw on the *North and South* Facebook group, there were some women reenactors in the film.

They're living historians. Reenactment is more actual physical fighting—reeanacting a battle. Living historians tell more of a story and show the way somebody lived. In these camps, women went with the troops to help set up camps. They cooked for them and cleaned and all other kinds of services. If you were an officer, you could take your family with you. Plus, women would go in groups and set up a laundry or food and make a living from it.

Anything else you can think of?

It wasn't like Patrick was trying to make himself the center of attention. He was trying to figure out what we were doing. Then when he lightened up and became his own self, he felt comfortable around us being the way he wanted to be (talking the way he wanted and stuff like that), to lighten his own tension. I don't care how professional you are, you get in these situations and a lot of pressure comes on you when you're trying to do your job right. You've got cameras all over you and you have big scenes and big lines, and that's a lot of pressure. You have to have a way to let that steam off so you can relax and do your job right. He had that down, and he helped us do it, and we helped him do it. It was just a lot of fun working with him because of that.

Credit: Warner Brothers/Kobal/Shutterstock.

Patrick Swayze as Darrel Curtis in The Outsiders, *the 1983 Francis Ford Coppola movie. Tom Cruise is back (left) and Rob Lowe is back (right).*

Credit: Bill EuDaly (Actor, *North and South*).

Patrick Swayze as Orry Main, in sword fight with Philip Casnoff as Elkanah Bent, in North and South *1985.*

Credit: Shutterstock.

Patrick Swayze as Orry Main, a Southern soldier, on the set of the TV miniseries North and South, *June 15, 1985.*

Credit: Artisan/Everett/Shutterstock.

Patrick Swayze as Johnny Castle and Jennifer Grey as Baby Houseman in the iconic finale dance scene of Dirty Dancing.

Credit: MGM/UA/Kobal/Shutterstock.

Patrick Swayze as Dalton, a Zen bar bouncer, in the 1989 Road House *film.*

Credit: Ray Cottingham, Stunt Skydiving Cameraman, *Point Break.*

Patrick Swayze skydiving as Bodhi in Point Break *(1991).*

Credit: Ray Cottingham, Stunt Skydiving Cameraman, *Point Break*.

Patrick Swayze and Kevin O'Donnelly (Director for the jump filming of Point Break*) at Perris Drop Zone.*

Credit: Ray Cottingham, Stunt Skydiving Cameraman, *Point Break*.

Patrick Swayze skydiving as Bodhi at Perris Drop Zone for Point Break.

Used with permission of Timothy Linh Bui.

Patrick Swayze as Jim Lance and Timothy Linh Bui, Writer and Director, on the set of Green Dragon.

Credit: Hopper Stone, SMPSP. Used with permission of Timothy Linh Bui.

Patrick Swayze as Jim Lance and Don Duong (1957–2011) acclaimed actor as Tai Tran in Green Dragon.

Used with permission of Joshua Sinclair.

Patrick Swayze and Joshua Sinclair, Director, Writer, and Producer, on the set of Jump!

Used with permission of Joshua Sinclair.

Jump! *poster for the 2007 Joshua Sinclair film for which Patrick Swayze was awarded Best International Actor on May 16, 2009.*

Used with permission of Timothy Linh Bui.

Timothy Linh Bui, Writer and Director, and Patrick Swayze, as Velvet Larry, on the set of Powder Blue.

Credit: Frank Whiteley. Used with permission of Frank Whiteley.

Patrick Swayze and Frank Whiteley, longtime friend and bodyguard.

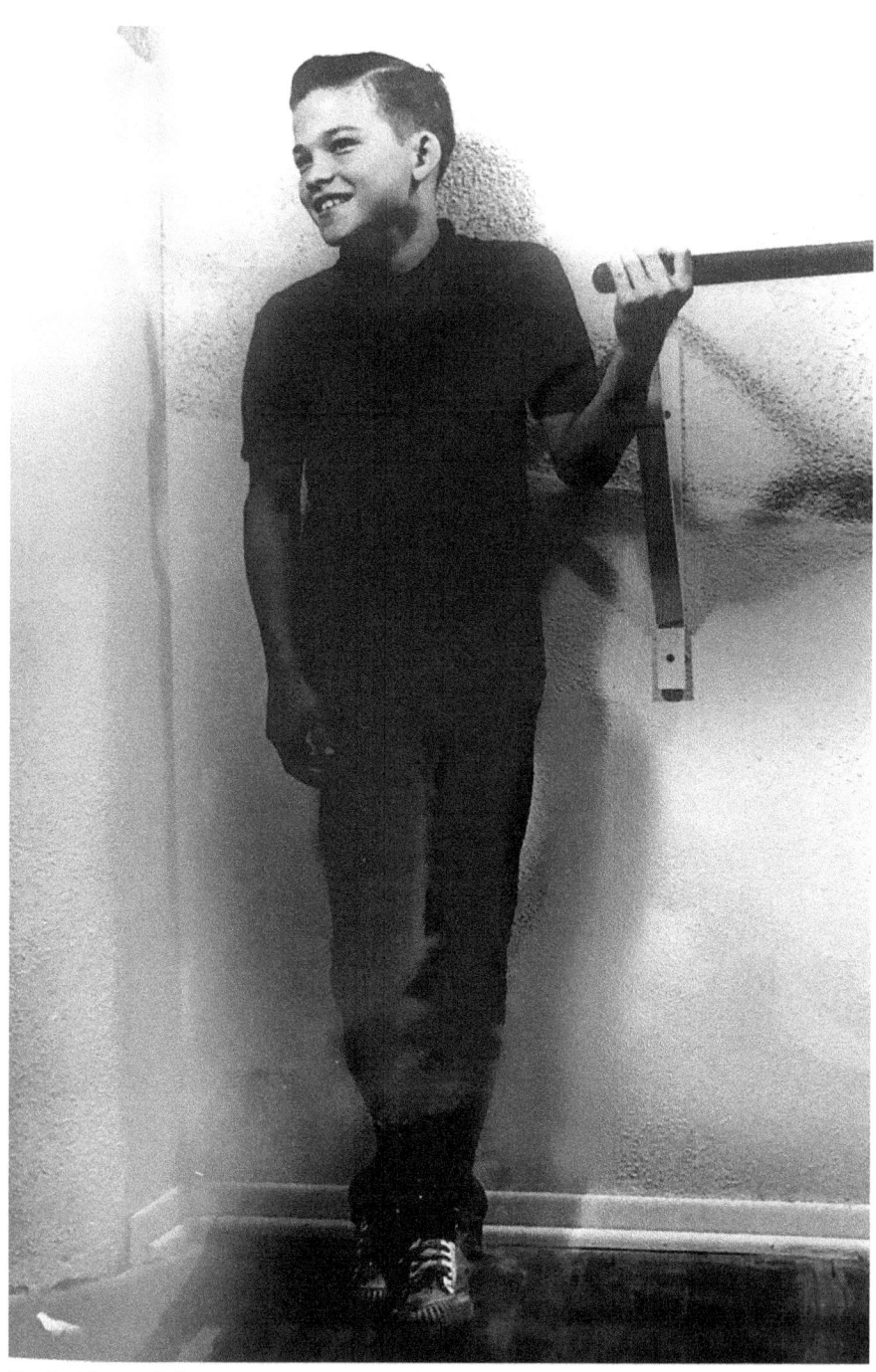

Used with permission.

Patrick as a child at the dance barre.

CHAPTER 3

ALL ABOUT DANCE

Patrick talked about what he got from his mother, Patsy Swayze, who was a world-renowned dancer, choreographer, and teacher:

> That's the other side of me: the intensity, the passion, the drive, the belief in communicating something through the arts. It's all those qualities of my mother's that have really led me down all these tangential paths in my life. My parents were an amazing couple.
>
> *Patrick Swayze, June 2004, From Alex Simon interview*

> **Patrick:** I was literally born on the stage, grew up with kings and queens and giants and fairies and goblins being my babysitters. Sleeping in theater seats from the time I was little 'cause my mother is a choreographer, so she's choreographed just about every musical ever written. . . .

Gavin Esler: What was it about dance that got to you? Was it the athleticism, the grace, or what was the spark there?

> **Patrick:** Well, you know, I don't remember a time not being in love with dance and music . . . There was something about when you step on stage, and something happens to you, and something communicates through you. I really believe dance is the truest form of communication. It's our oldest form of worship, from dancing to beating logs around a fire.
>
> I would have to admit that no matter how far I go as an actor, as much as I love my craft and I fall in love with it more and more as the years go on, nothing will ever replace the dance—'cause it's

that kind of communication that doesn't require the benefit or hindrance of words. If you can get to that place where you truly can communicate something, you know, through your body just with a simple move. It's a beautiful thing when you can hit it. . . .

The dance world teaches you something. . . . The concept of: Suffer for your art. Pay your dues. And then it takes me into Texas clichés. Only the strong survive. Nobody said it was going to be easy. If it's worth having, it's worth working for. I live by these things in my life.

Patrick Swayze, 2006, From Gavin Esler BBC HARDtalk Extra *interview*

CHRISTOPHER RIORDAN

Dancer, Actor, Choreographer, Director, and Friend of Patrick and Patsy Swayze

Telephone Interview: May 27, 2023

Thank you so much for granting this interview. I am collecting stories, memories and tributes to Patrick Swayze for my new book.

I know you were very close with Patsy [Patrick's mother] and she was a dear friend. I'm assuming that you met Patsy before you met Patrick.

Yes.

Okay. So for some backstory, how did you meet Patsy?

We both were members of an organization called the Professional Dancers Society. I became the chairman of the board of directors.

So Patsy was thrilled because, quite honestly, most dancers aren't great business people. Patsy was. I guess I knew what I was doing. Otherwise, I wouldn't have held that position for very long. What we were trying to do at that time was to get a home for retired and/or disabled dancers. It was very difficult because, as I said, dancers, per se, are not terribly organized. And they're always thinking of performing, or whatever, some sort of personal thing, more than trying to really help somebody else.

By that, I don't mean to be nasty or anything, it's just that it's not in their nature. Dancers are really rather self-centered. They have to be because you have to be concentrating on your body and what's going on with whatever it is you're working on. You know the saying, "No pain, no gain." Dancers are by nature very disciplined people, but in a sense, very self-centered. I don't mean that in a bad way; just that it has to be. You really have to concentrate all of your attention on yourself, your body, and what's going on within you.

Patsy and I got along very well. We traveled all over the country trying to raise funds and giving our name and what-not. We went to awards things.

We judged dance contests and spoke about dancing. The one time I really loved was when we were invited to go to Houston, because of course that was Patsy's hometown. They treated us like royalty, absolutely wonderful. Big limousine at the airport and a big sign: Patsy Swayze and guest. They loved her, you know, because after all, she did create the art center there. So they just were thrilled that she was coming back.

I was discovered by Fred Astaire. I don't know whether you know that or not.

No.

I was discovered by Fred Astaire to replace Fred Astaire. If you were a member of any of these dance groups, and this particular group was called the Ballroom Dancers Hall of Fame, so they knew who I was as well. I wasn't just somebody who was carrying Patsy's luggage or something. In fact, they carried our luggage.

Okay. Cool.

They were really absolutely wonderful to us. That was probably my favorite time of doing all this.

We had so many great conversations in the airplanes. Once you get up in an airplane, it's just the two of you. You'd better be interesting or have some good conversation. Of course, I had had many years in Hollywood, before she ever came to Hollywood, so I gave her all of that information. She, of course, told me what she was doing before she came to Hollywood. So that's how we met.

Every year, the organization for dancers used to give an award luncheon to somebody deserving. This one particular time, I think they asked if Patrick would come along. Patsy said, "I'm hesitant to ask Patrick because right at this particular time . . ." It was when he became really, really hot. So she said, "I am afraid people will swamp him. Sometimes these things get a little crazy. You know, some of these people will start grabbing at you and so forth." I said, "Patsy, why don't you take a table next to my table? My son is coming. My son Sean is taller than I am, so he's a bit formidable, and we can watch out for Patrick." So that's how I met Patrick, at that particular luncheon.

Oh, wow.

I saw him many times after that.

I had one time, I think this was in '89, I was producing and directing a television show called *Show Talk*, and this was having guests come and talk about their careers. This was not just dancers. This would be singers, and stunt people, and composers, and anybody who worked in show business; film especially, of course. I asked Patsy if she would like to appear on the show. She said, "Of course, I'd love to do that. Do you mind if I bring Donny?" I said, "By all means, please bring Donny." In actuality, I became closer to Donny [Patrick's brother] than I did to Patrick. Of course, Patrick was so busy with so many things. It was very difficult to get him to attend everything. The Swayze family, some of them have been to my home, you can't get any better than the Swayzes. They're just lovely, lovely people. It affected me greatly when we lost Patsy.

Aw.

She was just a great friend and very loyal.

We got into a bit of a mess. Some dancers, especially male dancers, can be very petty when it comes to getting credit. They would rather destroy something rather than be able to lose any kind of credit. And that happened to us when we were very close to getting the funds for the home for the disabled and retired dancers. They treated me very badly.

Oh, I'm sorry.

Subsequently, Patsy quit the organization. I, of course, left as well. She did go back to the organization when they decided they were going to honor Patrick. And I said to her, "I understand perfectly and by all means do that. Patrick's name deserves to be in the history books as being one of the recipients of the Gypsy award. Why not? It has nothing to do with me or anything else." That's how loyal Patsy was. She was just a great friend, a wonderful person, and we got along like brother and sister.

So about how many years were you friends?

I think we met in the mid-eighties. We met before Patrick had done *Dirty Dancing*.

Okay. That came out in '87.

I think we probably met around '85 or '86, something like that, and of course right up until she passed.

That's a long friendship.

Yeah, a long time. We just got a great kick out of each other.

I'm so glad.

She was just wonderful, a wonderful person, a giving person, who would always help somebody no matter what it was. She was right there volunteering and it has gone to her family as well. Donny's the same way. Patrick was very sweet and kind.

Bambi was a dear girl. I never really got to know Sean and Vicky well. Vicky didn't show up at very many things and Sean didn't either. Bambi came to the house. Donny and his wife came. I would see Patrick and his wife at certain functions, you know, Hollywood functions. Of course, he was always just very gracious. It seemed like he always remembered that I had volunteered to protect him. You didn't think of him as being this Hollywood sex symbol. I've known Hollywood celebrities practically my whole life. So it didn't surprise me that he was really a very down-to-earth person, especially knowing Patsy. You couldn't get any more down-to-earth than Patsy Swayze.

I can tell you that Patrick was totally devoted to his mother, as was Donny and the rest of the children, really. But Patrick just seemed to put her on a pedestal, and rightly so. She just was a really unique human being.

Did you ever meet Patsy?

I did, when they had the premiere of *One Last Dance*, the movie. It was in Houston. That was Patrick's and Lisa's movie. Patsy was one of the four choreographers of the film.

I used to be in Patrick's official international fan club. They organized a bunch of people to go to the premiere. People came from Europe, Canada, and across the states. We were sitting in the theater right in front of Patrick's family. They showed the movie. Then they had a reception at a hotel. That's where I got to talk to Patrick just a little bit. You can imagine, he was running around like crazy with no

bodyguard. That is where I got to meet Patsy. I might have talked to her for three minutes.

Oh, dear.

I was super-impressed. The other thing that happened was the very next day, we had a tour bus. We (all of the fans) were going to tour Houston. Patsy came on the bus. It was a really big surprise. She said, "Patrick is going to come on the bus. You can ask us any questions you want, but just please don't take any more pictures because Patrick's eyes are too sensitive from all of the photos from last night." Then Patrick came on the bus. You can only imagine. It was really great. Patsy and Patrick had a fun kind of banter while talking to each other. They stayed on the bus almost an hour. We just couldn't even believe it.

One of the ladies on the bus wasn't feeling well. She had to get off of the bus. You know what happened? Patsy went after her to check on her to make sure she was okay.

When I talked to Patsy the night before, she was very gracious. Even though I didn't talk to her for very long, I was just really impressed.

I'm not surprised that she did that, because that's just the way Patsy was. Unfortunately, I was living in Mexico at the time of that show. I remember her telling me about it. Well, we would write to each other. She couldn't understand what took so long for the mail to get to Mexico. I had to explain it to her. I wish I could have been there. I'm not surprised she behaved as she did because that was just her nature. She was very mothering.

Every year, the organization would also have a picnic. I would show up early because being the chairman of the board, I wanted to make sure everything was done properly. Of course, the one other person who would show up early was Patsy.

I'll never forget the first time this happened. I looked over and there she was, mopping this wood platform thing that was going to be like the place where dancers could perform. And I saw her mopping this, and I said, "Patsy, what are you doing?" She said, "Oh honey, don't you know, you really must mop these things with Coca-Cola so that you don't slip and fall." I said, "In all my years of dancing, I never knew that." And I have a picture of her, as a matter of fact. I took a picture of her with the mop.

Oh, wow! That is really cute. I remember you sent me, via Facebook, a picture of you and Patsy. That was really a nice picture.

Were we sitting at a table all dressed up?

Yes.

That was taken in Houston, the Professional Ballroom Dancers Society—very nice people.

Here's the photo. It says it's from 1991.

There's another picture that I really like. I think it was right after she was mopping the stage, as she called it. We were sitting down resting. It's a really very nice casual, candid shot somebody took. I don't look terribly good. My hair's blowing all over the place. Patsy, of course, had just finished mopping, so she doesn't look absolutely glamorous. It's just a nice warm, candid photo. If I can find it, I will send it to you. [See page 121 for photo.]

Is there anything else you can think of about Patrick?

It's always great, for me anyway, I love it when a dancer can break the ranks and make it. He handled it beautifully. He did not let his ego get in the way. He listened to his mother. She would give him advice about, you know, "I don't think this is the way to do it." He would say, "Okay, Mom, if you think so." I have a lot of respect for Patrick and the way he handled the success that came to him. When it was away from show business and it was all very personal, he just behaved beautifully, and of course that's due to his mother and father. I never met the father, but everything that Patsy told me about him and everything that Donny told me about his father, you can just tell that he was a wonderful man. They did a great job in raising those kids, believe me.

It seems like it.

Very much so. Yes.

I met Patrick four times. Of course, I met him in Houston that one time. Then he was in Detroit (I live just outside of Detroit). He was here twice to host a benefit for Complexions Contemporary Ballet—it was two fundraisers, and Complexions performed at each one. The

other time I met him was in Nashville at the film festival there, where *One Last Dance* was shown. Patrick was really great to his fans. I will tell you that.

Yes, I always admired him for that. That's the way you should behave, the way Patrick would behave. I try to do the same thing when I do all these Elvis things. [Christopher Riordan appeared with Elvis Presley in six movies, in Presley's first TV special in 1968, and in at least eight Presley documentaries. So he has been a frequent guest at Elvis festivals and events. Christopher was in many more movies, sixty-eight total, and received the Lifetime Achievement Award from the Los Angeles Motion Picture Council on October 13, 2014. He also has done over 250 television appearances since 1956; including being part of the *Batman* cast in 1966.]

And then I do a lot of autograph shows, too, for the Hollywood fan and the fan of movies. I am associated with so many different things, such as Fred Astaire, and of course just so many, *Batman*.

It is amazing, Christopher.

So I do a lot of these. They always say to me, "Oh, you're so nice to the fans." If it wasn't for the fans, who would buy the pictures? That's the way it should be. *You should really appreciate your fans.* So I'm glad that you noticed that about Patrick.

Oh, absolutely.

I always felt the same way about him, and Patsy would be the same way as well.

His bodyguard would be going, "Okay. Come on, we have to leave now." "No, no, no. I have to finish signing all of these autographs."

Yeah, exactly. That's right.

That memory was from Nashville.

In Houston, at that reception after the screening of the movie, he was just running all around. I would say there were around a thousand people there. Finally, there was some security with him. I met Lisa and I met her mother for a second.

I'll never forget that event in Houston, as long as I live. I'm sure the other fans who were there are the same way. I had never done anything like that before or since.

I still have a lot of friends—and they're all over the world—from being in Patrick's fan club and of course writing these books. So I will be forever grateful to him. The lady who was running the fan club is over in Scotland and we're still in touch. He was just a good guy.

He was.

He was very down-to-earth with his fans. I told him in Houston, "I saw you when you came to the Complexions event in Detroit." He said, "Now you get to see me dance in the movie." He did not dance in Detroit. He introduced the company and hosted the reception.

I was very lucky. I look back, and I go, "Wow, how did all that happen, exactly?"

I was just curious. You started at such a young age with your career. Were you taking lessons in dance and acting before you started?

Actually, I was just interviewed about this. Do you ever get the magazine *Films of the Golden Age*?

No.

You can still get a copy. They did a big article on me. They were asking, "How long have you been dancing?" and I said, "Well, let's see, this year will be eighty-two years."

Oh, wow!

Actually, I began working before I ever took any classes. Finally, I was at a point where I thought if I'm going to continue with this, I'd better start taking classes in different areas and learn what I'm actually doing. I didn't really consider myself a dancer. I considered myself an actor. I tell the story about when Fred Astaire saw me at a dance studio. He called me over, explaining why he wanted to hire me and everything. I was pretty young and really kind of stupid. I said to him, "But you know, Mr. Astaire, I'm not really a dancer." He put his hand on my shoulder and he said, "Kid, you're a dancer."

You were born talented.

I guess. It's something that I've always done. If somebody says, "Can you do this? Can you do that? Can you fall off the building?" "Oh, yeah. Okay, I'll do that." Just do it. I've been doing this a long time now. In fact, somebody asked me the other day, "How many movies have you been in?" I said, "I had to count all of this up when they did this article on me. I have done sixty-eight films and over 250 television episodes."

Oh, wow!

I have to be in Canada in July for another Elvis Presley festival. I don't know whether you know, I worked with Elvis more than any other person in film and television.

Awesome!

I was known for being his favorite dancer, so I am invited to these things all over the world actually, but a lot in Canada. Canadian people seem to love Elvis. It's always exciting and it's fun. Of course, when I'm there, I always say, "Who knew Elvis would still be paying me?"

That's hilarious.

It's not like my first day in the business or anything. It was quite an experience working with Hermes Pan.

Hermes was Fred Astaire's choreographer. It was Hermes who saw me first, and he got on the phone and said to Fred, "Get down here right now." So Fred came down. Hermes hired me for several other things. Right after we finished doing the Las Vegas show, he asked me if I was busy when I got back to LA.

I said, "No. Not really. Why?"

And he said, "Well, I'm going to be doing a movie and I thought maybe you might want to work with me again."

I said, "I'd love to." This was at a party, so we were being interrupted all the time. Finally, Hermes came up to me, and he said, "I'm leaving now, but I'll call you when you get back into town." I said, "By the way, what's the name of the movie that you're going to do?" He said, "It's called *My Fair Lady*." So I had six-and-a-half months of working on *My Fair Lady* [1964]. Then he hired me again for the Carol Channing special [1966]. I got wonderful billing with that because it's: Carol Channing and Christopher Riordan and fifty male dancers.

That's amazing.

Pretty nice. It pays to be with the top people, believe me.

I was going to tell you my favorite Patsy Swayze story. This was before caller ID. When you call somebody, they can see who's calling now. Years ago, they didn't have that. You've spoken with Patsy, so you know about her voice. [It was gravelly]. She would call and I'd run to the phone and say, "Hello?"

She'd say, "Christopher."

I'd say, "Patsy, hi. How are you?"

And she'd say, "How do you know it's me?"

That's hilarious.

I always get a kick out of that. She was such a sweet lady and not even thinking that she had any kind of identifiable quality about her. She didn't consider herself terribly special.

Really!

She considered her children very special, but she didn't consider herself terribly special. She knew how to dance and she knew how to teach. She was an excellent teacher.

That's what everyone says.

She knew how to get through to people. She had no ego. If you really got to know Patrick and got to know Donny, they didn't express ego at all. They just expressed that they were in the business and that they were hard workers. It was just: this is what we do. Very down-to-earth, very real people—I think that's why I liked them so much. There was no phoniness.

You have to understand, I've been in Hollywood now for almost seventy years. So I've known a lot of people. Do you know who Louis Milestone was?

No, I'm sorry, I do not.

Louis Milestone was the first person to receive an Academy Award, the first director to receive an Academy Award for directing and the first director to win two Academy Awards for directing. He became like my surrogate father. He and his wife sort of took me in and they would introduce me as the son they never had. Of course, my dad worked in films. He started in 1918. So you can imagine the people that I met who would come to the door, people like Charlie Chaplin and Ingrid Bergman.

So I'm not terribly impressed with names, but I'm very impressed with wonderful people, real people, and warm people, and sincere people. And that's certainly what the Swayze family had. I get a little choked up even thinking about all of the fun times that we had. Patsy and I had a lot of laughs.

I am so glad.

A lot of laughs. And Patrick appreciated that. He would often kind of tease me and say, "This is probably something you want to talk over with my mother." He knew we made each other laugh, big-time.

That's sweet.

He was a sweet guy, a very sweet man.

DWIGHT BAXTER
Choreographer, Director, Broadway Performer, Friend of Patrick, Former Dance Student of Patsy Swayze

Telephone Interview: October 15, 2019

These excerpts are from *Patsy Swayze: Every Day, A Chance to Dance* (2022) by Sue Tabashnik.

When did you first meet Patsy and under what circumstances?

I met Patsy when I was at the High School for the Performing Arts, back in 1971 or 1972. I was about twelve.

What did you learn from Patsy? How did she influence you?

What I learned from Patsy was simple: *Get out there and do it.* When you know the choreography, you know what you're doing, and then you know how to present yourself on stage.

She was a great influence on me. She is the reason I am where I am today.

Patsy was a go-getter. At that time here in Texas, segregation was still strong. The whole thing about Patsy, she was the only one who would allow Blacks to dance. All the other dance schools, they didn't allow that to happen. . . . Racial tensions were still very strong. . . .

There was a mission that they wanted to start at the performing arts school here in Houston, Texas, like it was in New York. So Mary Martha Lappe, Ruth Denney, Patsy Swayze, a lot of the leaders in the world of dance, even at the Houston Ballet, came together along with Bill Chaison, Eugene Collins (his wife was the prima ballerina for the Houston Ballet), and they all came to show us how it's done. If it wasn't for them bringing the company of the American Ballet Theatre, we would not have known what it was really all about.

At that moment, I saw Keith Lee, an African American, along with Mr. Arthur Mitchell, do classical ballet, Tchaikovsky's *Swan Lake*. That gave us the impetus to learn more about the world of dance. You know George Faison, the choreographer and founder of one of the greatest musicals in the world, *The Wiz*. George brought his dance company down there. That's when we saw Debbie Allen, who is from Houston, an alumna of Patsy's high school. She said, "Now you guys; keep doing it." She was at Howard University at the time. She is a little older than us.

Debbie Allen, Patsy Swayze, George Faison, Arthur Mitchell, Keith Lee, all those people were just good influences for us to understand the world of dance. We didn't know. A sixteen-year-old child doesn't really know what he wants to do. I took the liberty to say, "I want to learn this. I want to be a ballet master."

After I finished up with Patsy, I went down to New York and started studying with the Dance Theatre of Harlem.

So how old were you at that point?

I was seventeen. I went to Purchase College State University of New York, in the New York system.

Believe it or not, at that time, her [Patsy's] son, Patrick Swayze was my roommate.

When he was with the Harkness Ballet?

Yeah. Buddy was with the Harkness Ballet. We were roommates.

How did that go for you?

It went great, two Southern boys.

He was cool. Buddy was really cool. He married one of our close high school friends, Miss Lisa Haapaniemi. They became husband and wife. They used to do a lot of *pas de deux* together. It was just wonderful. We all just stayed close because we were all from Texas and we were all in New York together. You know, New York can be kind of unfriendly.

Tell me more about being roommates with Buddy.

He was a great person. We were cool together. We were at two different ballet companies studying dance, classical ballet. He was just a good person.

He was who he was when you see him in his movies, like *Ghost*. He went and did *Grease* on Broadway. Most people, when you say "Buddy," who are you talking about? We called him Buddy. *Dirty Dancing;* that's Buddy. When he did the *Road House* film; that was Buddy. He loved the outdoors. He had a ranch in New Mexico, Lisa and him. He was who he really was.

I miss Patsy to this day, because, you know, she's always been a great influence. . . . I mean she gave us a break. I wouldn't be talking to you today, if it wasn't for knowing what Patsy was all about and why God put her here on this Earth to say, "I'm going to teach you how to dance."

Sue Tabashnik

MORE FROM PATRICK ABOUT DANCE

After we finished the major push for *One Last Dance* after 20 years, then this incredible event that we did at the Joyce Theater that was a phenomenal Honour and opportunity for the Gala performance and fundraiser to be centered around *One Last Dance* and all our dancers. . . .

We've really turned into the spokespeople for the Dance World and the Arts World and we're doing tons of speeches. We've just finished launching the first Dance Festival on the West Coast in Laguna Beach, we just did an event for Dancers for AIDS and it was based on the future stars of tomorrow; these young dancers and young dance companies, so we are getting the opportunity to go out there with the Nevada Ballet and we can turn this into a life's work. . . .

Everyone wants us to do the same format that we did at the Joyce Theater—live dancers and then use their local dancers and with the film and benefit screenings, because it can bring in lots and lots of money to the Arts. It's something, we really, as much or more than Conservation, we have a passion about, which is our artistic sensibilities, and our creative abilities and passions are the only things that separate us from the beasts and make us special.

When you look at the United States, the United States are systemically eliminating artistic classes for kids! It's insanity. We're going to build generations of computers, soul-less computers. People don't realise that nurturing side of ourselves, nurturing that compassion, and that ephemeral and keeping that little bird alive and the child alive, which is the only way we resist cynicism and becoming jaded. Those are the things that nurture our passion about preservation, conservation, everything. It's like the basis of where the goodness in us began and the hope continues.

Patrick Swayze, November 27, 2005, From the Official Patrick Swayze International Fan Club interview

Courtesy of Nancy Schmidt.

Nancy Schmidt and Buddy Swayze. Love Story, *January 1973, at a dance convention in New York.*

Used with permission of Christopher Riordan.

Patsy Swayze (second from right) and Christopher Riordan (far right) after Patsy did her Coca-Cola mopping of the "stage" at one of the annual dancer picnics.

CHAPTER 4

SUPPORTING CAST

Patrick talked about his father, Jesse Swayze, who had ranching in his background and whose profession was engineering:

> He really taught me so many things that in your younger years are kind of cliché, but as you get older, you realize their importance: like integrity, passion, in your work ethic. I now live my life by most of the things my dad taught me. I think my favorite saying of his would be: All I got is my integrity. To this day, I ain't never seen a hearse pulling a U-Haul.

Patrick Swayze, June 2004, From Alex Simon interview

RACHEL M. LEON

Cousin

Written by Rachel M. Leon: May 24, 2024 (Edited May 26, 2024)

When I was five or six, my aunt Patsy was my dance teacher for like two years. She was firm and strict, but we spent time almost daily with Patsy and Patrick. I think she had a dance studio somewhere in the Heights. I was still young when Patrick moved from Houston to LA.

It was hard being his cousin because first, no one ever believed me. Second, well, my friends were "googoo" over him. I could never join the crowd because it was awkward. I couldn't be drooling over him because he was family. So I kind of felt left out, especially during the *Dirty Dancing* era. All the girls were going crazy. It was like they had their own little clique,

Patrick Swayze lovers. It really did bother me.

I do have a particular story about my time with Patrick. When I was twelve, my mom, who lived in California at the time and worked as a model, brought me to California for two weeks in the summer. I got to be on the set of *Road House*, where I got to meet Sam Elliott and Michael Wise, as they came to Patrick's trailer when he took breaks. They sat with us and we laughed and talked for about an hour. I was pretty starstruck.

LARRY WARD

Lifelong Friend

Telephone Interview: June 2, 2023

When did you first meet Buddy?

It was the summer of '65. I grew up overseas, in Egypt. We had just moved back. My dad bought a house. I didn't know anybody and I was on my bicycle on my driveway. Buddy drove by, stopped, and introduced himself. [We were the] same age.

How old were you?

Almost thirteen. His birthday was in August [1952] and mine was a couple of months later in October.

From there, we went over to his house which was around the corner. All of his aunts were there. I introduced myself. "I'm Larry Ward." "Is your dad Buck Ward?" It turns out his parents and my parents double-dated in high school. Yeah, they all knew my dad. So that was an automatic like, "Okay, you're in."

Do you have any favorite memories or stories?

There are several. We did kid things.

One thing that always cracked me up: Buddy was very competitive and so was I.

Back in the early days, he liked to play Tarzan out in the woods. We both grew up watching *The Rifleman*, a TV show starring Chuck Connors. Buddy acquired a .22 lever-action. I had a semi-automatic .22. He was telling me he could shoot faster than I could. I go, "No way, Buddy." So we got out in the woods. I showed him how fast an automatic was, and he said, "Okay."

As kids, I kind of ballooned out because I didn't know anybody and I stayed in a lot and ate. I got kind of fat, but he was still my buddy. I wasn't used to being fat. He was very streamlined. I'd go up to the dance studio and hang out. I guess my only real regret to this day is not taking dancing. I know a lot about it because I hung out there all the time. That's where the girls were.

Why do you regret not taking dance?

I really grew to appreciate it—the athleticism involved. I was a pretty athletic kid, but I was so self-conscious about my weight. I was embarrassed. That was the only thing that kept me away from it.

We were both big and athletic for our age, so nobody really messed with us. He got into martial arts. Once we were wrestling in their living room and he threw me over his head. It was like, "Oh!" and that made me want to take martial arts. I did, later on in life. I spent a lot of time doing that.

I think Big Buddy [Buddy's father, Jesse] was a Golden Glove boxer at one time. I remember Buddy and me going to the dance studio to put on the gloves, and Big Buddy was the referee. We had a couple of other people to box—fun stuff.

Buddy was extremely [talented in] gymnastics. I'd get on a trampoline and I was nervous just to jump up and down. He was doing baranis [aerial somersault flips] and backflips and all kinds of stuff. He, and a trampoline and a diving board, it was pretty special. He had dynamic coordination.

Didn't he have a college scholarship for gymnastics?

I know he went to San Jac junior college [Patrick attended San Jacinto College in Pasadena, Texas on a scholarship for gymnastics] and I went off to Albion Junior College. I went to play basketball. He left San Jac and then I think he went up to New York to do ballet.

Were you still in touch then?

We remained friends our whole lives.

One of my favorite stories . . . actually two stories. He was living in California. He had a ranch there with Lisa. I was in the neighborhood and called him up and went over there and we visited. He had just gotten back from doing *City of Joy* [1992] in Calcutta. *Point Break* was about a week-and-a-half away from coming out. So we're in his studio in his house and he was showing me clips from *Point Break*, the skydiving stuff.

Oh, wow.

So we got all excited. The next thing I know, we're driving to Perris, California in my company truck. We get there. It was the last flight of the day. The lead guy goes, "Buddy, we only have room for one." He points to me. You're supposed to go through this long orientation, but they just dressed me and we're running out to the airplane. It was a DC3 and the guy's hollering instructions and I can't hear a word because the plane's engines are on. The next thing I know, I'm at 13,000 feet with the sky behind me, jumping out of an airplane. I got on the ground, and said, "Where's Buddy?" "Well, he chartered his own plane."

Oh, my gosh. So with no orientation, you jumped out of a plane!

The other story that was so funny. I worked a graveyard shift and I called him up and said, "Can I come crash at your place?" "Oh, sure." So I get there. We visited a little bit. He'd just gotten a Harley-Davidson. He knew I rode. He threw me the keys and he goes, "When you get up, come over to this house. I want to show you this house I'm restoring." So I get up and get on the bike and drive over there and he's out on the street talking to this red-headed dude and this blonde from Austin. He introduces me. She's from Austin and that is where I was living. So I proceeded talking to this guy for thirty minutes telling him about the music scene in Austin. We had a nice visit. We said, "Goodbye" and they walked next door to this mansion.

Buddy saw that I had a funny look on my face, and he goes, "You know who that is, right?" "Yeah, he said his name was Joe." "That's Joe Walsh." Here I am spending thirty minutes telling Joe Walsh about the music scene.

And Buddy just let me talk.

That's cute.

He invited me to do a round-up with him on his big ranch, the two thousand-acre ranch outside of Las Vegas in New Mexico. He goes, "It depends if I take this part in this series called *The Beast*." Well, he took the part.

That was right before he was diagnosed?

I'm not sure when he got diagnosed. I talked to him. He was telling me that he had some issues and he was going to fight it.

He sure did.

Yeah, he did. He had trouble keeping his weight up and things like that.

Yeah. Do you think his fame changed him at all?

I don't see how it could not, but he tried to stay as level as he could. I'd read these articles in these magazines, and I'd call him up and go, "Buddy!" He goes, "It's Hollywood." For me, he didn't really change that much. I don't know how that would be for somebody else since we go back to such an early age. There wasn't much he could do. I was very, very happy for his success.

Another one he did for me. He was going to be at the Houston Livestock Show and Rodeo and sing with the Gatlin brothers. He and Lisa were staying at the Astra Hotel, so he invited me and my wife over. We followed him over to the Astrodome. So we're behind the scenes. I knew he was popular, *but I had no idea how much* until he rode that horse around. [I was] watching all the girls almost die trying to reach over the rails and stuff. I go, "Whoa!" He did his thing.

Backstage, his dressing room was down this long, dark corridor. So I'm walking down the corridor to go talk to him. The guy next to me is Larry Gatlin. I don't say anything. I get to the door and I knock, and Buddy goes, "Who is it?" I go, "It's Larry and Larry, and we're looking for Darryl." So everybody got a chuckle out of it. I saw Gatlin at Buddy's wake and I didn't think he would remember, and I said, "I know you don't remember me." I told him the story, and he looked at me, "That was a long time ago", and he remembered it.

It was a real pleasure having Buddy around the corner. Patsy was welcoming and open to everybody. There were all kinds of people there all of the time. They made you feel at home. I was going over to the house all of the time back in our high school days. I always stayed in touch with Patsy and went out to California to visit her and things like that.

That's sweet.

I think a lot of people would say she was their second mom.

I just did a book on her, which was published last summer [2022]. A lot of the women would say that, a lot of her students.

She taught a very select, very talented group, Cookie Joe and Nikki D'Amico, and a bunch of them.

Donny (Buddy's brother) was like a little brother to me. Buddy's first cousin, Jimmie Ingram, is one of my closest friends. Then it goes back to the days when Vicky (Buddy's sister) was alive. Bless her heart. I was there when Bambi (Buddy's sister) first arrived from Korea. She was four years old. She didn't speak any English. We had a Korean friend [who helped translate].

Another story that I just remembered. Buddy and I went to get our motorcycle licenses, so he had borrowed a little bike from a friend. Back then, I had a car. Buddy went first. Buddy was a good rider, but the policeman wanted things done in certain ways. Anyway, I'm taking note. Buddy failed and I passed. That was another one he did not like. I would have failed, too, if I had gone first. I would have done pretty much what Buddy did.

Obviously, eventually he got the license.

Oh, yeah. I think he had a 750 Honda up there in New York forever.

There are a lot of photos of him on a motorcycle.

I had a car and he didn't. I helped him with his paper route in high school, just to earn some money. We'd get up early in the morning and load the car with papers.

To be so young again! How did you guys have so much energy to do all you did: school, sports, paper route? And he was dancing, too.

That's what I have to give Buddy. He managed to make good grades and be very active in sports. Of course, he excelled as a dancer. I do believe if he hadn't had his knee taken out during the second-to-last football game in high school, that he was a Baryshnikov-caliber dancer. That knee injury really messed him up.

I think he really managed it as well as possible.

I think he did. I forgot where I got the information from (whether he told me), but when he was doing *Dirty Dancing,* that jumping off the stage was really, really hard on him.

What they talk about in a documentary [*The Movies That Made Us: Dirty Dancing, 2019*] is that he jumped off the stage around twelve times in the finale scene rehearsal. Reportedly, he then said to the choreographer, Kenny Ortega that he could do it only one more time. And of course, he did it, and the rest is history.

Yeah, he did it—a very determined individual!

One of my favorites . . . Buddy was just getting really popular. He's in town. Jimmie, his cousin, and me were at Leanna Sparacino's, and we kind of pulled an all-nighter.

Well, you know, he had to live his life, too. I think Leanna's daughter, Heather, told me about that night. She was only about nine years old then.

Exactly, if that.

She said she woke up and Buddy said, "Don't worry, I'll make you breakfast."

That sounds about right. She could have been younger than nine.

Somebody who made a big impression on Buddy was Tom McNair.

He was the expert with the horses, right?

Yeah. Rhita [his wife] just passed away a couple of days ago [May 30, 2023].

I'm sorry to hear this.

She was a great lady, too.

On a personal level, Buddy took me over to their ranch. When I first met

Tom and Rhita and the gang, we're in the trophy room. They're all sitting on the couch. I'm up walking, looking at pictures. I look at this one horse, and I go, "Is that Sultan?" And they froze. Someone said, "How do you know that horse?" I go, "I used to ride him." Their jaws went to the floor.

My understanding was the lineage started with Sultan, with Tammen and everything else. Sultan was the horse. It was in the stables in Egypt. They let me ride him occasionally—not out by myself. He was *the* horse in the stables.

What kind of influence did Tom have on Buddy?

My take would be, Tom set a saddle better than anybody I've ever seen. So he made Buddy a better cowboy, a better rider. He educated him. They were big on Arabians and Buddy got into Arabians, which was cool.

I rode the white horse [maybe it was Kuyhaylan Roh—Tammen x Alleyah]. I didn't ride Tammen.

Some people say Buddy was more into the horses than into the movies.

I think he did get to that point. We weren't really talking back at that time. The follow-up on that was he was doing a lot of shows. He was just so proud of Tammen. He loved his animals. He was crazy about Cody [his dog who died from cancer in August 1995].

He was an actor. He was famous. I think he used that to his benefit with horses because his passion became horses.

Then in *Point Break*, he showed me a bunch of the surf boards that he used. When we were kids and I had the car, we'd go to Galveston to go surfing.

I thought he had never surfed before *Point Break*.

Well, I mean you have to understand, it's Galveston. We had these big giant boards and we'd catch whitewash and that was pretty much the extent of the surfing.

What's whitewash?

You know when the wave kind of folds out and turns white. In Galveston, there's not much to catch. But, you know, we wanted to be surfers.

The level in *Point Break* was some serious stuff that would have been all new to him, I'm sure. He had the athleticism and skill-set to run with it and be successful with it.

I talked to several of the camera stuntmen from *Point Break* about the skydiving. They were very impressed with Buddy, how he could just do that. I think that was pretty new to him.

Yeah, he got into that for the movie. He did his own skydiving stunts and air acrobatics.

Like a dancer in the air.

Quite impressive!

Back in high school days and living at home, you didn't cross Patsy. If Patsy said, "Be in at twelve," you didn't come in at 12:01. We'd come in like two minutes late and Patsy was in Patrick's face and his jaw was tight, and I'm going, "See ya later."

Everybody loved Big Buddy, but you didn't cross him. He was such an easy person to be around. After *Urban Cowboy*, Big Buddy was excited about having a country-western bar he opened up called the Lazy S Saloon. They had a cast party for *Urban Cowboy* and Travolta and a bunch of them showed up. I remember going over to Gilley's and meeting just about everybody in the cast, except Travolta.

Wow! I guess Patsy taught Travolta the two-step.

Ah-huh. I get a kick out of the movie because of that scene where there's dancing—there's a bunch of people, like Leanna and Jimmie, who are in the background. Jimmie was at a table or something.

He was in *Road House* too, right?

Jimmie was in *Road House*. Well, actually, they had a scene with him, but they didn't use it in the movie.

That is too bad.

Which was way too bad. Jimmie and I dubbed it and sent it to Buddy's Aunt Kitty. She just got the biggest kick out of that.

Another story: Buddy was my friend, but when a movie came out, it just wasn't me to go be the first in line. So I went out to visit him at his ranch.

You know, in *Road House*, the Mercedes-Benz?

Yes.

In the movie, it's blown up, but it really wasn't. He bought it for Lisa. I get there, and I go, "Hey, nice-looking car." "Don't you recognize it from *Road House*?" I hadn't seen *Road House* yet, so I go, "Oh, yeah." I had to go see the movie.

I'm glad you had all of that time with him and have all of these memories.

That's a life-time. It changed my life a bit, being his best friend.

I never asked him for anything, except one time. People at the office I worked at knew that I knew Buddy and wanted to go see Jay Leno in LA. They didn't know how to get tickets. I told them I would make a phone call and that would be the extent of it. I got a hold of Patrick's secretary and asked for tickets for *The Jay Leno Show*. She said, "That's the hardest ticket in town to get." "Okay. Thank you." Thirty minutes later, she called and said, "Let me work on it." Thirty minutes later, she goes, "I got you four tickets." I have a feeling that either Buddy or Lisa made sure it happened. I really appreciated it.

What about his music—playing guitar, writing songs?

I remember back in high school days, he had a nice Gibson guitar. I just remember we'd sit in his bedroom and listen to a lot of Simon and Garfunkel back then. We went to the theater-in-the-round in Houston to see The Association. After the show, we're talking to one of the members of The Association. He said, "You all stay for the second show."

I don't remember The Association.

[Larry sings] Cherish is the word . . .

Ok, I know now. Thank you. You didn't know you'd have to sing for this.

[Laughs] That was the other thing, Buddy always had the leads in all of the musicals. I was in a couple in the chorus because it was fun. He could sing and dance. They did *West Side Story*—boy, he nailed it.

I'm not surprised.

That's what he did.

Out of all of the five Swayze kids, why did Buddy become "the star?"

He was a good-looking man, very athletic, all of the dancing. I think Donny is a fabulous actor . . . but he didn't do all of the dancing stuff. Buddy and Donny were tight.

How many years are they apart?

Five. My little brother and Donny were good friends and the same age.

Sean [Patrick's brother] and I kind of stay in touch.

That's good.

I have a question for you. How did you get interested in Buddy?

Way back in the *Dirty Dancing* days, I just fell in love with that movie. It was sort of a rough time in my life. I thought it was overall an optimistic movie. When I saw Buddy in *Dirty Dancing*, oh my goodness! Then what really did it for me, what nailed it for me, was when Barbara Walters did that interview way back in 1988. He was talking about his dad and he's crying and he says he wants to honor his dad by having a ranch. I just became a super-fan. I've never been a fan of anyone else, before or after.

I ended up joining the Official Patrick Swayze International Fan Club, and that may sound kind of hokey. Margaret, in Scotland, was president and running the club. I became involved in the club. To this day, I still have friends because of Buddy and the club.

Buddy came here, to Detroit, twice to do a benefit for Complexions Contemporary Ballet. Complexions does dance outreach with inner city kids and they did it in Detroit. I'm not saying that Buddy personally did the outreach; the company executed it. He was on the Board of Directors—so was Lisa. Complexions did a performance and Buddy hosted a reception afterwards both times, to raise money for Complexions.

There were a lot of people there for both events, 2002 and 2004, but I got to talk to him a little bit each time. My aunt Nedra was with me for the first Complexions benefit because she was a big fan of Patrick (although not as intense as I was) and his movie *City of Joy*. The way he was when he met my aunt and me, and how he handled everything, just really impressed me.

Now don't get me wrong, I was not like best friends with him. I was a fan who met him four times and followed his career. Buddy and Lisa would send updates to the fan club on projects and events.

I went to the premiere of *One Last Dance* in Houston in 2003. Were you there?

No, I had just moved to Pittsburgh, I think.

Let's say about thirty people from the fan club attended and some came from Europe. Margaret traveled from Scotland and people were there from other European countries, Canada, and from across the US.

Buddy took the time to take photos with the fan club group. He was running around at the reception after the premiere with no security [detail] at first. There were around a thousand people there. He talked to me a little bit. I told him, "I met you in Detroit at the Complexions benefit," and he said, "Well now you got to see me dance!"

I met Patsy for a few minutes at the reception. She came on our fan tour bus the next day. We had hired a bus to take us on a tour of Houston to where Patrick lived growing up, where he got married, where the dance studio used to be, and other places. Patsy got on the bus and told us Patrick is going to come on the bus. She said, he asks that you please do not take pictures, as his eyes are really sensitive from all of the photos the night before. She told us we could ask questions. We're like, really! Our fan club president had set it up. Patrick and Patsy stayed on the bus almost an hour and we could ask any questions we wanted. People mostly asked about his movies and how he met Lisa. How many people with his fame would do that?

I was writing articles for the quarterly fan club magazine—actually around thirteen articles. In Houston, I got very inspired by Patrick. The movie *One Last Dance* is about making your dreams come true. That is when I decided to write a book. People have asked me, "What author inspired you to become an author?" I'd say, "It wasn't an author. It was Patrick Swayze." He was just full of energy and life.

A friend of mine had said, "You are going to meet Patrick" and I told her that she was nuts. I mean, I don't think he was a God or anything, nobody's perfect. He would be the first to tell you he wasn't.

My grandmother died from pancreatic cancer. That's just such a bad, bad illness. I thought how he handled it was just amazing and courageous.

I talked to his co-star Travis in *The Beast* at the wake for quite a while. He said due to Patrick having the pancreatic cancer during the series, he was often in a lot of pain. He would do his role. That's all you can do, I guess. He did everything he could to make the show work, but he was in a lot of pain doing it.

I know years ago, when Patrick asked my opinion about *Red Dawn* [1984], he quit asking my opinion after I told him.

Really!

I really enjoyed *Red Dawn,* but I think it had one big flaw. To me, if they would have had a prom and developed the characters before people started dropping out of the sky—something where you get to know the people.

I think my favorite performance is *City of Joy*. It was a humble role. It wasn't bad-ass or anything like that. I thought *Ghost* was very good, too. *Three Wishes* [1995] and *Tiger Warsaw* [1986] were well-done—it's not the macho stuff, it had more character to it.

Yeah. He did so many performances—movies, TV shows, Broadway shows. It's amazing all that he did. Personally, I can't watch his stuff sometimes. It's too emotional for me and it's too sad.

I got a kick when Buddy goes to Hollywood and everybody moves to Hollywood. Patsy's out there and I went to visit her. I said, "Patsy, what do you think about Hollywood?" "I hate it." I go, "Why?" "Nothing but *sunshine* every day."

That's hilarious. I started off as a super-fan and now I am an author. I get something out of it just by writing.

That's a wonderful thing.

I will tell you that Buddy's courage for what he had to face with pancreatic cancer made a big impact on me. I would think about my situation and that would help me get through it. I think a lot of people noticed his courage and have been positively influenced by Buddy.

He adopted his role, which was who he was. Everything he attempted, he'd go at it head-on to win. When he got the cancer, he was going to go at it head-on and beat it. We talked about it. "I'm just going to beat it." Unfortunately, that's a tough one.

By the time you get diagnosed, it's too late, in many cases. They misdiagnosed my grandmother several times and when they finally got the right diagnosis, she died three weeks later. That was many years ago. I was reading the other day that there are some new possible advances for diagnosis and treatment of the illness. I really hope so! That would be so good.

Oh yeah.

Did I answer your question?

You did, very thoroughly.

I have a friend, Joshua Sinclair who wrote, directed, and produced *Jump!* which was Buddy's second-to-last movie. Joshua flew into Detroit from Europe and we had a fundraiser for the Patrick Swayze Pancreatic Cancer Research Fund at the Stanford Cancer Institute via the Jewish Film Festival. I never would have become friends with Joshua if it wasn't for Patrick. You know what I mean?

I do . . .

The last time I spoke with Buddy was right before *The Beast*. We talked for about two hours just catching up. He was telling me about how weird it was being famous. It was a good, long conversation. We caught up and made plans that never happened, but the intention was good.

Sue Tabashnik

MICHAEL PASCOE

Friend, Dance Student of Patsy Swayze

PATRICK AND ME

Written by Michael Pascoe: July 4, 2023

First time I met Patrick Swayze was at the first rehearsal for *West Side Story* in 1981. We got to know him as Buddy. He played the lead, Tony. His mom choreographed and directed the production that was done in Moorpark, California. Patsy rented a small studio space on Los Angeles Ave in Simi Valley, California where she lived with her husband, Big Buddy. And that's where we would rehearse.

Part of the set for the show was a wire fence that was permanently placed on the stage. During the scene where Tony stabs Maria's brother Riff (who is Tony's best friend, played by Patrick's brother Donny), Tony grabs him to run away. I still remember Patrick hurling his body over that fence. I swore that he would get hurt, but he never did.

One day we were practicing the fight scene for the Rumble and Buddy gave us tips on what to do. He showed us the stuff he learned on the movie sets. After we went over it a few times, he was not happy with the intensity involved. He pointed to me and my fight partner, TJ. He told them that was how it should look like.

I got to be friends with the family at that point. During one of the rehearsals at Patsy's new studio, she turned on the TV and we watched the television series *M*A*S*H*, the episode [Blood Brothers—1981] with Patrick. All of the girls cried, "Buddy died!"

We were proud of him, always hoping he would go far.

One of the characters, who played Baby John, had a little brother named Kevin that tagged along during rehearsals. He was so little and cute, Patsy fell in love with him. She thought of an idea to have him hang around the Jets and be the little brother of another character in the play named Diesel. We named him Piston. Buddy also liked Piston.

During the run of our show, Buddy was hired by Francis Ford Coppola to be in the movie about the book *The Outsiders*. This took a while to cast the film, rehearse, and then have the final product finally released in 1983.

After *West Side Story* closed, Patsy had kept the studio space that she rented to rehearse the show and turned it into her first dance studio in California.

I do remember one day Buddy was coming back from the early casting days of the film *The Outsiders* and he talked about it with Patsy. He told her that Francis needed an actor to play his baby brother, Ponyboy. He thought Kevin would be perfect for it. But Kevin was too young for the role. So Patsy remembered a friend of hers from the *Urban Cowboy* days who was a rope spinner and stuntman. She knew that his son, Tommy, was an actor, so she suggested him [C. Thomas Howell].

The movie might have been released in 1983, but it took a while for it to be made. How Buddy found time to do other projects, I have no idea. His manager, Bob LeMond, wasn't sure of which direction to take his career; films or TV. Buddy scored big in *M*A*S*H*, then was cast in a restyled *Mod Squad* kind of show called *The Renegades*. If the show did well, then Buddy would have been a fixture on TV.

I got close to his dad Jesse (Bud) Swayze. He was known simply as Big Bud. He had a dry sense of humor and always seemed to come up with the perfect whimsical phrase. In 1982, Simi Valley police told Patsy that her husband Bud, the love of her life, died of a massive heart attack. The family was devastated.

When he died, we were all sad. The family took it hard. For the funeral, I dressed up in a suit, but the family dressed casual, just as their dad would have wanted it. Patrick saw me in the suit and wanted to know why I was dressed up. I told him I cared about his dad a lot and that was how I wanted to respect him.

Patsy and the family carried on. She would divert her pain by diving full-time into her new studio. She always had certain ways of motivating us to do better.

When the pilot for *The Renegades* came out, everyone in the studio saw it.

The TV show never took off, and instead, the movie *The Outsiders* did. It boosted Buddy's career.

John Travolta's manager Bob LeMond molded Patrick's career. He died [on August 8, 1986] before Buddy became a star, but was responsible for putting him at the right place at the right time. Though another manager took over, it was Bob's earlier work with him that helped catapult Buddy's career. Patsy told me that Buddy was on the set doing a movie when he found out about Bob's death, and John Travolta was there at the same studio, and they both cried. Bob discovered John, and so he was very close to him.

We didn't see much of Buddy after that because he was busy doing all of those films.

Up to this point in Patrick Swayze's career, he was typecast as thugs and ruffians who were always fighting against the system. Patsy was proud when Patrick was cast as Southern gentleman Orry Main in the TV miniseries *North and South*. This was Buddy's biggest part to date. He not only had the lead that carried the story, but it was broadcast on a major network.

Buddy wanted to get back into dancing and started to attend classes. Simi Valley was too far for him to attend classes on a regular basis. So, because of its location, he was only able to come to North Hollywood, where his mom was teaching at Debbie Reynolds Studio.

The first class back, Buddy walks into the studio. He sets his dance bag down, and skips warm up. Now, he hadn't danced in a while. He goes to the center of the floor, and does a double *tour en l'air*. I was blown away. I was only able to do a single, and not great at that.

How he could just go into fifth position, *passé* his leg from the back to the side into fifth front, take off straight into the air, straight as a board, and then come down so gracefully? And at the same time, made it look so macho. He was like Gene Kelly in that way.

He was always in the dance studio after that. I got even closer to him. Buddy had a great sense of humor. He would talk about upcoming projects, but never had that arrogance like he was better than you.

Eventually, he got back into enough shape that he was offered the role of Johnny Castle in *Dirty Dancing*. When Patsy heard the title of the film, she was dead set against it. It was a good thing he didn't listen, because it was one of his biggest films ever.

He could do anything and everything he set his mind to. If he wanted to write music, he wrote music. One time, he and Lisa were fixing up an old ranch off of the 210 in LA County and wanted all of us at the studio to help him. He made a day of it, feeding us and made it seem like a backyard family picnic.

He was telling us about a keyboard machine he bought that helped him write his new song. He played it for us and it was "She's Like the Wind." Who knew at the time it would be such a big hit? But, hey it was Buddy—he could do anything.

Patsy, too, got involved with everything she could. She was thirty years older than me, but I couldn't keep up with her. She was staging a show for someone who had a nightclub for kids. After our classes at Debbie Reynolds' on Saturday, I would tag along and assist her.

Marc Lemkin owned the club and wanted to do a video to capitalize on the *Dirty Dancing* craze. He asked Patsy not only to do it, but have her son Patrick do a cameo. Well, with Buddy, there was no cameo. When he came to do his shot, he improvised the entire scene at Patsy's office at the dance studio. His personality really showed through.

When we did the filming at the Red Onion restaurant in Woodland Hills, California, Buddy was not there. The scene of him giving the students the thumbs up was added later.

The last time I worked with Buddy was when he did a benefit that was held at his sister Bambi's high school in Simi Valley, California. That was also my Alma Mater. It was a variety show and Patrick Swayze would be the feature. I was supposed to do my magic act and had my table with my props set up in the wings.

Patrick went on before me. He was so jazzed performing in front of a live audience that, when he came backstage after his set, he ran smack dab into my table, knocking it down, breaking it. He apologized, but I had to do my act with the table top lying on the stage floor.

I moved to Vegas after that and met my wife and we opened our own dance studio. When we got married, I invited Patsy and Buddy, but because of prior commitments, they couldn't come. They did send us their best though.

I never saw Buddy again, but followed everything he did. I was so sad when he got cancer, but was convinced that he would beat it. He fought bravely, but eventually, the cancer took a great spirit.

The world was lucky that it had Patrick Swayze in it, but sad when he left oh too soon. *His kind only came around once in a blue moon.* I am glad, Sue, that you reached out to me for this interview. I was so delighted that I knew this special person. He always made you feel like you were his best friend.

VICKI MANCUSO

Friend, Dance Student of Patsy Swayze

Written by Vicki Mancuso: April 2, 2023

I'm going to share with you my two favorite Buddy memories. These two things show, beyond any reason, what a beloved person he truly was.

FIRST STORY
In 1968, I was almost eleven. My mom was an alcoholic and wasn't as present as Mama Patsy was for the things young girls go through. I was very skinny and really plain and had very little confidence.

There was a girl I went to school with as well as dance class. She was a bit of a bully and she seemed to love taunting me with the fact that her mother was always around. She sewed all her clothes and was so proud of her dancing. (She was an okay dancer, but very mechanical). Anyway, she got pleasure out of reminding me my mom wasn't really there for me. Many times, I stayed with Mama Patsy after class because she would take me home some days and others I would go home with her and eat before going home. So one afternoon, I was sitting on the floor changing my shoes when Buddy came over to me and squatted down in front of me. He said, "Little Bit, don't pay attention to that girl. If things were so great, she wouldn't be trying so hard to make you feel bad." He lifted my chin up and made me look at him. He leaned in, and said, "You're going to be a knockout in a few years. You're already beautiful—you just don't know it yet." He winked at me, and walked off.

Mama Patsy apparently saw and heard the exchange and she came over and hugged me, and said, "He's right, you know." That one exchange, first with Buddy and then with Mama Patsy, gave me something I didn't even know I needed. Encouragement from them made a huge difference in the way I saw myself for years to come, and confidence, too.

SECOND STORY

The second story is priceless and I'll never forget it no matter how old I get. My mom had stopped drinking cold turkey in January of 1976. I'd been feeling terrible pain in my side, but it was my senior year and I was still dancing and was an officer in the drill team. I passed out from the pain one morning and ended up in emergency surgery. Due to complications, I had three more surgeries in one week and didn't get out of the hospital until the end of April. It was a terrifying time, but my mom never left my side, and I honestly don't think I would've survived if not for her love.

As time moved us forward, Mom became my best friend, but in 2005 she was hospitalized with congestive heart failure complicated by her type 2 diabetes. Mom was in and out of the hospital for the next four years and in early April 2009, she slipped into a coma and remained in one for a week-and-a-half. She and Mama Patsy had stayed in touch, and I know they talked several times over the years. That's how I found out Buddy had cancer.

When Mom called to tell me about Buddy's cancer diagnosis, I was scared for him. My grandfather died of pancreatic cancer in 1968 . . .

On April 19th, Daddy called me at work and said, "Mama's awake, so I'm going to hold the phone so she can talk to you." I was thrilled at hearing her voice. She was very weak and emotional, but she told me how proud she was of the woman I'd become and she said, "I love you." That was about three in the afternoon. Daddy said that she was very tired and weak and that I should wait until the next day to go see her.

I went home around six and did my regular routine and was lying in bed reading when Daddy called again at nine-thirty. He was crying and said, "Vic, Mama's gone. She had a heart attack in her sleep." He said he was going to stay with her until the funeral home came to pick her up. I was devastated. All I could do was sit there and cry.

My phone rang about eleven-forty-five and I was stunned to hear Buddy's voice. He said, "Little Bit, I wanted to see if you needed anything. I'm sorry for your loss. Barbara was an amazing woman to stop drinking the way she did and she taught you how to be strong." I was still in shock, but I asked him how he was feeling, and he said, "Well, you know me, I'm fine." (Typical Buddy) I remember telling him how much I appreciated his calling and he told me he'd never forget the special people in his life. He then said, "You need anything, just call. Love you, Little Bit."

About two weeks later I found out that on the day my Mom died, Patrick had just found out his cancer had spread to his liver. That was April 19, 2009. With all he was going through, he was thinking about me losing my mother. Up until that day, the last time I'd spoken with him was 1990, while I was living in New York, and before that, it was 1986, just after my husband and I moved there.

And in 2013 Daddy died of it [pancreatic cancer], too. Three months ago, I had my own scare of pancreatic cancer. I went through the biopsy and other tests, and thank God mine was negative. But I did have pancreatitis.

Buddy was an incredible, perfectly-flawed man who didn't forget the people he cared about. I miss him always.

NANCY SCHMIDT
Friend, Dance Student of Patsy Swayze

Written by Nancy Schmidt: May 21, 2023

I did have the pleasure of being one of Patrick's dance partners for a time, such as for the *Raymonda Ballet* and *Love Story pas de deux*. Just know he was one of the best dance partners one could ever have!

PATRICK SWAYZE Still Inspiring!

FRANCIE MENDENHALL

Friend of Patrick and Patsy Swayze, Dance Student of Patsy, and Performer in Shows Choreographed by Patsy Swayze

Telephone Interview: May 19, 2020

These excerpts (edited on May 11, 2023) are from *Patsy Swayze: Every Day, A Chance to Dance* (2022) by Sue Tabashnik.

I met Patsy's son, Patrick/Buddy while being taught how to climb a high wire for the musical *Carnival*! [Patsy was the choreographer.] He decided I was just the bee's knees, and asked if I'd go steady, and I said, "Sure."

Then this boy in the show who I saw every day decided he liked me, too, and I thought, I am really confused. I am going to tell Patrick that I can't be his girlfriend. Patsy told him and returned the disk to her son. He had given me his disk with his name on it, which was the thing you did at the time—you know, something to wear around your neck.

I went to school and I did the show. I went home and I went to sleep. I went to school. I did the show. We were twelve.

I saw Patrick decades later when he was here in Houston honoring his mother Patsy at Theatre Under The Stars. Once I reminded him who I was, he looked at me like, "See!"

Sue Tabashnik

HEATHER SPARACINO CRANE
Friend, Dance Student of Patsy Swayze

Telephone Interview: May 11, 2023

So your mom [Leanna Sparacino] said you had a story about Buddy to share.

I grew up with him. I remember going out to his ranch and riding around on the tractor with him in Simi Valley [California] when I was nine.

He used to come into town to Houston [where I lived as a child]. Apparently, there was a night of adulting (no kids allowed) and I woke up the next morning to everybody asleep in the living room and my mom was still asleep. Buddy said, "Don't worry about it, I got it for you. I'll make you breakfast." He made me a bowl of cereal.

He made you cereal?

He did. I asked for breakfast and he said, "What do you have? You don't have any eggs or anything, baby." And he made me cereal.

How old do you think you were?

Somewhere between five and eight years old.

How often did you see Buddy?

When we lived in California, I saw him regularly because we lived with Patsy. So I saw Buddy, Donny, Sean, Bambi, and Vicky regularly. Patsy had a chihuahua named Taco with a bad leg. He used to chase me around.

When did you move from Texas to California?

After third grade, I was out there for the year of fourth grade. I turned nine that summer in July. When fourth grade was up (I guess that was May or June back then), we came back to Texas.

Patsy used to have a house in Simi Valley with a swimming pool. We lived with her.

Did you take dance?

I did from Patsy. I think at the time Patsy was teaching at DR—Debbie Reynolds. I met Nell Carter (not sure if her last name was Carter at the time) from *Gimme a Break*. We, my mother, Lisa, and I were taking classes. I took pointe, ballet, tap, and jazz.

Oh wow! Do you still dance?

No, there's no real living in it. I went into medical sales. Now I'm into commercial landscape sales.

I'm going to send you some pictures. One is Buddy (a headshot) signed: *To my little lady. Love, Patrick Swayze*. I even have a picture of me with John Travolta.

How did you get that?

Patsy was the choreographer on *Urban Cowboy*. So I was out there with my mother. John Travolta bought me a Cherry coke at Mickey Gilley's.

Anything else about Buddy?

He walked into a room. He had a smile. You could have just lost your phone, your car, and your husband. He looks at you and smiles or says hello or gives you a hug, and you just forget about everything.

Such an amazing soul!

He seemed to, sort of no matter what was going on with him, be there for other people.

Yes.

I didn't see Buddy again after we left California when I was nine.

KATHERIN KOVIN-PACINO
Friend and Colleague of Patsy Swayze

Telephone Interview: October 2, 2020

These excerpts are from *Patsy Swayze: Every Day, A Chance to Dance* (2022) by Sue Tabashnik.

What was it like to work with Patsy on *Silver Foxes*?

Patsy was fun and energetic and she always shot from the hip. It was fun to hear her speak so fondly of her children, especially Patrick and Donny who, as you know, were both in the business.

What do you remember most about Patsy?

Patsy worked with the movie stars on many big films, including the John Travolta movie and of course, with Patrick, her own son [on *One Last Dance*].

I remember most her stories about Patrick and how he went to school on the first day and told her, "Mom, I was the handsomest guy in the class." She goes to her husband, Patrick's father, "He's an actor."

Did you ever meet Patrick?

I met Patrick and Donny, very nice gentlemen, nice Southern boys. They were very well brought-up, loved the family. That was very nice. I always liked Patrick (I only met him maybe two times) because he was a very sweet guy, very well-loved in the entertainment business.

Some people that I interviewed have said they thought Patsy and Patrick had similar personalities.

Yeah, the energy about him and you knew what he was thinking. A very nice guy. He just loved what he was doing in the industry and he was enthusiastic, and I liked that. It's good to see.

CHAPTER 5

THE FILM CRITIC AND THE ENTERTAINMENT JOURNALIST

JOE LEYDON
Film Critic

Excerpt from ***"Patrick Swayze: Back in Houston"***
By Joe Leydon: December 19, 1988, *The Moving Picture Show with Joe Leydon (movingpictureshow.com)*

Swayze and his wife have a ranch in the sprawling foothills surrounding Los Angeles. It's more than a great place to raise horses, or record music in a private studio, or work on their joint efforts in dance productions. It's also great therapy.

"We're trying to finish this barn at home, amongst traveling and doing benefits, and that kind of thing. It's exciting to see the ranch starting to come together. It looks like a desert now, because it's all dirt. I just spent three days straight on a bulldozer, on a tractor, finishing up all the final grading and stuff. That was actually real good for my head, to come home and go right back to that kind of work and just sort of settle myself back into being normal."

Trouble is, it's hard to keep Swayze down on the farm after the public has seen *Dirty Dancing*. He recently completed back-to-back movies—*Road House*, an action drama directed by Rowdy Harrington (*Jack's Back*), and *Next of Kin*, a police thriller co-starring Liam Neeson (*The Good*

Mother)—and is contemplating production deals with Columbia and Tri-Star. He has been offered opportunities to direct movies—"B-movie stuff, on a small level," he explained, modestly. And record companies, impressed with his success as singer and co-writer (with Stacy Widelitz) of "She's Like the Wind"—have been dangling contracts before him.

But Swayze remains cautious. Even after *Dirty Dancing*, he realizes that he still needs to prove himself as a "bankable" actor. Two films he made before *Dirty Dancing* was released, *Steel Dawn* and *Tiger Warsaw*, were box-office flops, even though they were released after *Dirty Dancing* hit big. "One hit movie does not a movie star make," Swayze said. "So, actually, from a career point of view, I need *Road House* and *Next of Kin*, one or both of them, to be hits."

As for working on the other side of the cameras, Swayze isn't ready to direct—not yet, at least. Nor is he quite ready to start recording albums.

"I've been offered album deals with just about every major label in Hollywood. But I turned them all down, because I don't want to look like just another actor trying to capitalize off an acting career, and stick himself in everybody's face musically.

"I've been writing music too many years, and music means enough to me to where I'll do it for [myself] in my little studio at home, or in my hotel room, and never let anybody hear it if I have to. I won't sell out on that part, I won't just start writing commercial tunes for the sake of making the buck, or selling an album."

Excerpt from "Patrick Swayze on 'Road House'"
By Joe Leydon: May 14, 1989, *The Moving Picture Show with Joe Leydon* (movingpictureshow.com)

This excerpt includes Joe Leydon speaking to Sam Elliott on the *Road House* press junket.

Sam Elliott (*Mask, Murder in Texas*) co-stars in *Road House* as Dalton's lean, leathery mentor. . . .

Elliott emphasized his great respect for Swayze.

"I love this kid," Elliott said. "I mean, I love this kid. I think he's a good actor. And he's a good guy.

"And there isn't anybody (in Hollywood) who can physically do what this kid does in this movie."

ALEX SIMON

Entertainment Journalist

Excerpt from **"Patrick Swayze: 1952-2009"**
By Alex Simon: June 10, 2015, *The Hollywood Interview.* "Great Conversations: Patrick Swayze." Originally published in the June, 2004 issue of *Venice Magazine (https://thehollywoodinterview.blogspot.com)*

Goodbye, Patrick. Thank you for always staying down to Earth, even when Hollywood tried to cast you out among the stars.

Excerpts from **"PATRICK SWAYZE: PEACEFUL WARRIOR"**
By Alex Simon: June 10, 2015, *The Hollywood Interview.* "Great Conversations: Patrick Swayze**."** Originally published in the June, 2004 issue of *Venice Magazine*
(https://thehollywoodinterview.blogspot.com)

Patrick Swayze has always been his own man. As early as 1979, when the former dancer and stage actor made his big screen debut in the roller disco opus *Skatetown USA*, Swayze easily could have let himself be packaged into that year's teen idol. But despite his cover boy looks, Swayze refused to be pigeonholed as flavor-of-the-month, and persevered as a serious actor, until 1983, when Francis Ford Coppola cast him, along with a crew of other unknowns with names like Tom Cruise, Emilio Estevez, and Matt Dillon in a little picture called *The Outsiders*. When he landed the lead in the hit miniseries "North & South" two years later, his stardom was solidified, and Patrick Swayze became another "overnight success," whose single night of paying dues lasted over a decade. . . .

Alex Simon: Speaking of "chick flicks," let's talk about *Ghost*.

Patrick: That, for me, was another testament that when you get people believing they're doing something special, something special happens. Jerry Zucker, being renowned for his comedic work, brought a wonderful thing to this project. And the writer, Bruce Joel Rubin, was a real gift because Bruce is a very spiritual man. When we'd be talking during the re-writes, we'd go into deeper topics about spirituality, but we finally came up with the idea that if you truly love someone and then you die, you take the love with you, because that's all you can really take. By curbing the desire to try to say too much, and thus possibly alienating people, and going back to very simple truths, it just seemed to resonate with a lot of people around the world. It was one of those films that come along and an alarm goes off in my body, telling me that I have to do it. It passed what I call "the goosebump test." When that happens, I know I have to do a film.

CHAPTER 6

THE FANS

"Fans have been so faithful and been behind me for so long, he says. I'd like to believe it's because I never forget that fans are the people who put you where you are at. I really appreciate that, and I've been able to have a career that keeps going and going and going."

Patrick Swayze, July 2004, From Greg Hernandez interview

JAN GRIFFITH

Written by Jan Griffith: May 28, 2023

I had the privilege of meeting Patrick Swayze twice. The first time was at the Nashville Film Festival on April 30, 2004 with two of my fellow fan club members. We were in Nashville to see *One Last Dance,* Patrick and Lisa's dream project. At the festival, they both introduced the film, then we watched the film (it was one of the first times it had been shown). Following the film, there was a question-and-answer session with Patrick, Lisa, and Stacy Widelitz. One of my favorite stories from that night was given by Stacy, who was the composer of the music in the film. One of the fans asked if Patrick and Lisa fought like their characters in the movie. Patrick and Lisa deadpanned a response that "No, they never fight." It was obvious they were being sarcastic, and it was hilarious to watch them banter back and forth. Stacy remarked that he remembered quite vividly arguments occurring like that in his home during the scoring of the film. We all laughed because these two passionate people obviously loved each other a great deal, so they fought, too.

Patrick, of course, being Patrick, had to stay to sign autographs. That was the first time I got up close and I got an autograph. My dear friend Sue Tabashnik pushed me forward so I could get an autograph in my program. Patrick remarked several times, "Just a few more" as he signed paper after paper. He was determined to sign as many autographs as he could. He always took time for his fans. He eventually glanced at his watch and said he had to go, that Lisa was waiting. We then went to a bar, BB King's, to listen to some great music and to get to meet Patrick and Lisa through the fan club. (As fan club members, our fan club president would get in touch with Patrick's personal assistant and arrange for fans to meet Patrick.) I'm not sure how much I remember exactly of this fantastic night. But what I remember most about that night at BB King's is that there was great blues music playing, and the kindness of Patrick and Lisa's personal assistant, Sheree. We were able to get her attention, and she came over and greeted us with, "Hey, you must be from the fan club." She asked us to give them [Patrick and Lisa] a few minutes to finish their drinks and probably to unwind a little after the film festival. I remember watching Patrick and Lisa out of the corner of my eye, butterflies fluttering in my stomach.

A few minutes later, we were led over to the section that had been reserved for Patrick and Lisa. I wish I could say that I was super articulate, but no—I was starstruck. I met Lisa first and then Patrick. While I do not remember what exactly was said, I do remember his quiet, "Hi" and a warm handshake. His hands were huge, but so gentle. It was loud in the club, but I recall just standing next to Patrick and listening to him talk. I am sure I looked like a little sister staring at her big brother. I have always thought of him like a big brother. At one point, Patrick turned and wrapped me in a big bear hug. I was shocked, but remember that he was built like a rock—all muscle—and I never felt safer. Looking back at that moment always makes me smile. We then took pictures to commemorate the event, and we had a wall of people watching. I asked Patrick how he did this all the time. He just laughed. We took several pictures, then more handshakes and hugs, and we said goodbye.

What I remember most from that night was the banter, the laughter, and the genuine caring I felt from both Patrick and Lisa. Patrick adored his fans and would spend a long time signing autographs, answering questions, allowing them to meet him and take pictures with him.

About a year later, April 25, 2005, I got my second chance to meet Patrick. This time I wasn't starstruck and was actually able to talk. This time we were at Fort Hood in Killeen, Texas. Patrick and Lisa were there to promote *One Last Dance* and to meet with some of the soldiers serving there. We met up with a fellow fan who got us on base and then waited in line in the PX because I and another fan, Shirley, had already met Patrick, Lisa, and their personal assistant, Sheree, in Nashville. We went up front first to make sure she knew we were in line. She actually asked us if we wanted to cut the line and go and meet with Patrick and Lisa first, but we agreed to wait in line, which is what we knew Patrick would have wanted. When we finally made it to the front of the line, Sheree went up and told Patrick and Lisa who we were. As we stepped behind them on the little stage that had been built for them to sign autographs, I made some comment about Sheree being the real one in charge, and that got a laugh from Patrick and Lisa. My favorite picture from that day is everyone is in profile except for me. I'm staring straight at the camera with a big smile on my face and everyone's looking my way. (It was taken right after my comment).

We didn't get very long that day with Patrick and Lisa. I asked Patrick how he liked flying the Apache helicopter simulator. He said the flying part was easy, but the weapons were hard; there were just too many buttons. After we took our photo, Patrick squeezed my hand as I was getting ready to leave the stage, and I told him that *One Last Dance* had inspired me to learn to horseback ride, which I ended up doing the next summer. I love riding as much as Patrick did. There was nothing better than being on the back of a horse. As he once said, when you're riding, you have to be completely in the moment. You can't be distracted or thinking about other things in your life. It's just you and the horse; and he, of course, was right.

We did get to hang around and watch them sign autograph after autograph and take picture after picture without stopping for hours. I also got some time to talk with Sheree outside the PX and even got to try on Patrick's flight jacket and take a picture wearing it. The story behind that was when they left Los Angeles that morning, it had been kind of cool and Sherry had forgotten a jacket. Patrick had grabbed his flight jacket out of the back of the car and tossed it to her telling her to wear it. I love that picture—for just a minute, little sister got to wear a big brother's jacket, and it didn't have

Patrick on the name tag, it said Buddy.

What I mostly remember about both meetings is how kind and funny Patrick was. I don't think his humor ever came across quite so well in interviews. Maybe he was too serious and too focused on promoting whatever film or show he was doing at the time, but he really was quite funny and so kind.

Both meetings revolved around *One Last Dance,* which is about fighting for your dreams and never letting them go. I think that's what I remember most about Patrick; he was a dreamer. He never stopped dreaming. And he never stopped learning. He was never satisfied with how things were and he was always willing to work hard to achieve whatever he wanted.

For me, Patrick Swayze was like a big brother, a model of who I wanted to be like—hard-working, kind, driven, and passionate. I carry those lessons with me each day in my own life. He was a great man; talented, caring, and most of all, honorable. His example continues to inspire me each day to reach for my dreams and to work hard to achieve them.

CRYSTAL L. BERGER

Interviews (email and telephone): January and July, 2008

When did you first see *Dirty Dancing*?

Summer of 1989.

So *Dirty Dancing* wasn't the first movie you saw Patrick in?

Yes, it was.

Why do you like *Dirty Dancing* so much?

I fell in love with Patrick's voice. I had heard the song "She's Like the Wind" in London, playing everywhere. My neighbor told me about the movie. I rented DD and fell in love with the whole movie.

I remember the era. I was too young to be part of it, so *Dirty Dancing* let me live vicariously. It was an age before our world view became more cynical. It resonates with me.

Dirty Dancing lets me get away from life's problems and takes me to a place I feel safe. I fell in love with the entire cast: Baby, Johnny, the dancers—the casting was perfect.

It has been a lovely friend through many years.

How has *Dirty Dancing* impacted you personally?

It helped me through my cancer treatment. I mentioned that I loved *Dirty Dancing*, and the nurses related to it. They knew what I was talking about without any explanation. (Interestingly, the nurses were twenty years younger than me.) They played the music for me. They talked about how wonderful Patrick was in this movie. We could go somewhere else besides the radiation room during my treatments. It was something positive in a difficult situation.

It kept me from moping and dwelling on things.

In addition to *Dirty Dancing*, how many movies have you seen multiple times, and is Patrick in them?

I haven't watched any other movie multiple times. DD is like a nice cup of tea and a good book on a rainy day.

Have you ever met Patrick or anyone else from the cast?

I met Patrick in Houston (2003) when *One Last Dance* was premiered. He was very gracious.

In Houston, did you get a chance to tell Patrick about *Dirty Dancing* helping you with your cancer treatment?

No, cancer was after Houston (January 13, 2004–2005).

I will always be grateful to Patrick Swayze and DD for helping me through this cancer. It is odd. I found the lump in my breast in LA the night two friends and I were going to see Patrick in *Chicago*. So I guess the Swayze will always be part of me, so to speak. . . .

Dirty Dancing and Patrick Swayze bring happiness. They are a happy jinx.

Sue Tabashnik

CLAIRE GREGAN

Written by Claire Gregan (excerpt is from an email interview):
January and November 2008

Have you ever met Patrick or anyone else from the cast of *Dirty Dancing*?

When I was a six-year-old girl at home one weekend, my mother's friend came round with a video for them to watch. I was told that it was a little too old for me to watch, but being the nosey six-year old I was at the time, I didn't give up, and I sat and watched the film with them. It was that rainy Saturday that I fell in lust with the one and only . . . Patrick Swayze! After that day and up until this day, I think I have seen the film nearer to 600 times, and I'm now twenty-six. I know the whole script—word for word! Dare I admit it! So from that Saturday, I was always found sitting watching *Dirty Dancing,* and I made a promise to my dad that: "When I'm a big girl, I'm going to America to find and hunt Patrick down!" That promise I made, I'm sure everyone, including my dad, heard on a day-to-day basis.

My dad used to come home with the huge posters of Patrick from the music store . . . Crazy things that mean so much when you are growing up and have an idol! Since then, I have seen every film that Patrick has filmed, joined the fan club, and most importantly, that dream that the little six-year-old girl had those years ago came true in 2006, when I met the man who I grew up adoring and admiring.

It started on the 5th August 2006. I was going to London with my mother and stepfather to watch the West End production of *Guys and Dolls* that Patrick was starring in. I'd seen the advertisement on his website and knew that was my chance of making that little girl's dream come true. So I booked the ticket and we set off from Preston Lancashire to London. As soon as he came on stage, I was totally amazed, shocked, couldn't believe he was there a few feet away from me. The show was amazing, but that wasn't enough.

After the show, we raced round to the stage door where we waited for an hour, and then there he was, standing right in front of me, talking to the crowd, all to be over too soon. I never got my chance to say a few words to him face-to-face. Heading back to Lancashire, I was still in shock that I'd seen the man I had idolized for the last nineteen years, but I still wasn't satisfied. So I went back, with my friend. I drove all the way back—the 300 miles—and got there early to the stage door to wait for Patrick to arrive. But he was held up in a traffic jam on the way to the theatre. I was informed by his bodyguard that he would be rushing back to go onstage, so we had to go and take our places inside, but he would get Patrick to sign my program for me.

Inside, we watched the show and came out early before it finished, to go back to the stage door to get my front row position to see Patrick—when he came out to chat to the crowd, as he did after every production. Once again, I was talking to the bodyguard. He was very friendly and agreed to get my book signed by the man himself.

Patrick again came out to talk to the crowd and I was standing at the front. I waved my hand in his direction and he came over and shook my hand. He spoke to me—asked my name. Amazing! I had done it. Patrick then went back through the gates and people were starting to leave. I stood there with my friend, upset that the bodyguard had not done as he'd said and gotten my program signed. So upset and deciding where to go next, his bodyguard came over to me, and said he needed a word with me. I was so very worried as to what maybe I had done wrong. I stepped forward to be taken through the electric gates to the stage door. As they opened—standing right in front of me was Patrick Swayze—looking right back at me, Claire Gregan, the girl with a dream from nineteen years ago. *So you see, dreams really do come true.*

This is just an insight to my story. I went on to date Patrick's bodyguard, met Patrick, and spent time and shared several occasions with himself and his lovely wife, Lisa, and the cast and crew of the production.

I wanted to tell my story. As silly as it is probably to some people, that was my dream, and I had made a promise that one day I would meet my idol. Although it didn't take me to America that time to hunt him down (guess he saved me a flight fare), I got there in the end, and that was the best three months of my life.

It all started back one rainy Saturday afternoon with a six-year-old girl. And now my four-year-old little boy is amazed by the film. He knows all of the words to "(I've Had) the Time of My Life" and is planning on following in Patrick's footsteps. The film means so much to some people.

I hope you do not mind me sharing my dream with you.

REGINE

Written by Regine: 2016

Patrick is my hero. This is for so many reasons. I am thrilled because he is so very talented. Is there anything he can't do? I don't know of anything. He always kept going; he never, ever gave up. He really loved what he did. He was so passionate and always gave more than 100 percent in everything he did. And his fight against this cancer was so brave. He never held back his emotions. He was so honest—so adorable.

Written by Regine: 2023

I do love Patrick and this will never stop. I am thinking of him every day and still enjoying all his wonderful work!
Dear Patrick, You will live in my heart forever!

Credit: Rob Hess.

Patrick Swayze with his beloved Arabian horse Tammen at the All Arabian Horse Show.

CHAPTER 7

MORE ABOUT ARABIAN HORSES: STARRING TAMMEN

"I feel like my soul gets to fly when I am with him."

Patrick Swayze talking about riding his horse Tammen in an episode of Wildlife, *an Australian TV series hosted by Olivia Newton-John, Human Nature, 1994 [Beyond Productions Pty Ltd]*

"I grew up with horses. My father was a cowboy in Texas. We lived in Houston. At the age of eight, I visited [Douglas Marshall's] Gleannloch Farm and from then on I was lost! I dreamed of nothing but Arabians, and when I imagined Arabians, they were Egyptians!" Swayze said in an interview.

"When you get a bond happening with a horse, it's interesting. I was raised a cowboy and did some rodeos and stuff and thought I was a horseman. Found out I knew nothing. As I have gotten into these horses, [Arabians] I have realized how far you can go with them," he said in 1994.

When asked what attracted him to Egyptian Arabians, the star of *Ghost*, *Dirty Dancing*, and *Road House* said: "Their beauty. I like the form of the head, the proud trot, the harmonious physique. Everything fits together and is in accord. There is a natural balance in everything. I am a dancer, and I can tell when a body is made with function in mind. A healthy Arabian is built for function! And that fascinates me."

Patrick Swayze quoted in a Horsetalk.co.nz article written on September 14, 2009

"I have a real passion and love for these horses. They have the ability for friendship and recognition and a relationship more than any other horse."

"Racing to me is a heritage in this country and in this world that I think is very, very important to never lose. The further we get in this high technological society, the further we get away from our roots and the further we get away from that very special, powerful bond that can exist between a man and a horse, or a man and a beast."

*Patrick Swayze, from a video interview hosted
by Bob Bork at the Sam Houston Race Park, September 13, 1997*

PATRICK SWAYZE Still Inspiring!

PAUL KOSTIAL

Founder and Executive Director of We LOVE Arabian Horses

Telephone Interview: March 21, 2024

When did you first meet Patrick and under what circumstances?

I have to think about what year it was, but I was competing in Western Pleasure. My area that I competed in was where my home was, where I grew up with my family in Houston, Texas. He was a competitor with his horse in Western Pleasure also and we would be at the same horse shows together. It would have been in the late seventies, early eighties, something like that. He would be at these horse shows and he was already famous by then.

The one show I remember in particular is the Houston Livestock Show and Rodeo. The fans were hanging over the rails while we're trying to compete in this Western class. He and I, and others, were competitors in the same class. If I recall correctly, I won that class. He came up to every single exhibitor later and apologized for all of the disruption.

I don't know if you know about horses.

I don't.

The Western Pleasure class is very calm and it's supposed to be very relaxed. A lot of paparazzi and cameras and screaming girls would not be what you would want to have happen. So it [Patrick's presence] increased the degree of difficulty for the competitors fairly significantly because it's supposed to be quiet. It was just a lot of disruption.

Anyway, he found every exhibitor and talked to us personally and apologized. Some people kind of knew him a little bit better. I didn't know him too well then. I knew him, but we weren't buddy-buddy. There would be more shows after that where he would always apologize to us.

It really wasn't his fault, sort of. Right?

It wasn't his fault, but we have other celebrities who have had similar situations . . . Usually at some point, it gets to be so much . . . that they just quit going to the horse shows, because they can't really go out into public without having this mess of people.

Horse shows are real congested. There are a lot of moving parts and a lot of people moving back and forth. You want less disruption.

He was very, very visible. Sometimes they would set up what's called the trail course for the horses to compete over. Patrick might be one of the volunteers out there helping set up the trail course.

Okay—that sounds like him.

He was very kind, very friendly, always so helpful, and always so apologetic [about] whatever was around him in his notoriety that was causing a disruption. He was very, very well-liked and very visible in our community.

So eventually, he stopped showing horses or competing. Right?

Yeah. . . .

The one horse he is most famous for—so if you're a researcher, you've probably heard of Tammen.

Yes.

They had other horses, but Tammen was kind of his favorite and kind of his big Arabian claim to fame. He would take Tammen to all the shows. Tammen was very special to him.

There's a picture out that was done decades ago, obviously. Patrick has his shirt off, but he's facing away from the camera, so you see his back and his arms are going from left to right from the front to the back of the horse, and the horse is Tammen. And he's holding Tammen, but you kind of see Patrick's muscle: back and shoulders and arms, holding the horse. It's a very iconic picture of Patrick. I'm sure it's easy to find.

I have that hanging up here.

I figured. It's kind of one of those real famous pictures of Patrick, at least one that is horse-related.

My understanding was that the poster of that photo used to be sold to raise money for the Arabian Horse Association for scholarships for

youth riders. The AHA doesn't sell the poster anymore. I got this poster years ago.

Now, for somebody who doesn't know much about horses, can you talk about the Arabians?

Sure.

Wonderful.

[First] one thing to go back to about Patrick. During those years when he was still very involved and visible at our national championship show every year (which is held in October), Patrick would sometimes carry the American flag, which was part of the opening ceremonies, on a horse that would be donated to him to use during this presentation. And they galloped and they've got the flag. And they do—it's called *turns*. They stop and sing the national anthem, also. One year, they have Lee Greenwood, and the next year, they might have Patrick. So Patrick was real involved in a visible way in those kinds of things, too, which are real crowd-pleasing events that go on at horse shows. He was always willing to do those kinds of things.

I saw a tape, and I think it was somewhere in Houston, in which Patrick came out riding with the American flag and then I think Patrick and Larry Gatlin were singing later.... [It may have been the Houston Livestock and Rodeo Show.] A friend of Patrick, Larry Ward, talked about being at the Houston Livestock and Rodeo Show. Did you know Larry?

No. I was young; I was late teens, going into college right around all this time. Patrick, I think, was a few years older than me. What year was he born in?

1952.

Patrick was nine years older than me. I would have been eighteen or nineteen probably in that class that I told you about at the Houston Livestock Show and Rodeo. He would have been twenty-seven or twenty-eight. He was more of an adult and I was kind of finishing my junior career. We were close enough in age that he would talk to all of us like we were just part of his friends. He was very, very polite and nice like that.

So what about the Arabian horse do you want me to tell you?

What makes the Arabian horse special?

Well, the Arabian horse is a very unique in breed because it's just so kind, gentle, and sensitive to its rider and its owner and its people. It kind of connects to you like you would think of a dog connecting to you. It's a little more that way than some other horse breeds, where it's just more attuned to its owner and it's very relational, so to speak. If you come into the barn, the Arabian horses are probably going to get up out of their stalls and nicker at you and look at you down the hallway until you come visit them or bring them their feed. They're very versatile, kind, and very disciplined horses that are very attuned to their owner.

When the Bedouins had Arabians for centuries in Saudi Arabia and Egypt, the Arabians would sleep in the Bedouins' tents with them. They were considered war horses and the primary possession of the sheik. The other horses would not be inside the tent like that. They were considered very protective of their owners. They were such a prized possession they got to be inside the tent, instead of staying outside of the tent where the other animals might be.

Oh, wow!

So Patrick was a hundred percent into Arabians. Both he and Lisa were very, very involved through all those years with their own horses. A gentleman by the name of Tom McNair was Patrick's trainer. Tom really didn't take on a lot of external clients because he worked for a very wealthy family in Houston named the Douglas Marshall family and they owned Gleannloch Farms. Somehow, Patrick became friends with Tom and Rhita, his wife, and they would take care of Patrick and train him. Both Tom and Rhita are deceased now, but his children are around, Dan and Maggie. They would have been friends with Patrick also.

What do you think Patrick contributed to the Arabian horse world?

His love of Arabian horses was so authentic and genuine. His passion for Arabians was very, very visible to people. Even today, when we put up pictures of Patrick on our social media or share stories, people are very interested in that story and anything around him. He was always considered very congenial and a contributing member of the family of Arabian horse lovers around the world.

He was just super-nice and involved and talked to people and didn't go hide, even with all his celebrity and stardom. It was long past the *Dirty Dancing* movie. He was very visible with everyone in the community. He just had such a deep, honest, very visible love of the Arabian horse.

There's a video of him speaking at a racetrack down in Houston. Tammen is in the video with him. He's holding Tammen while he's giving a speech and he talks about why he loves the Arabian horse. It's just such a from the heart kind of message from a human being sharing about why they love a certain type of animal. [Please see the beginning of this chapter for an excerpt of the video.]

Wow! I think I saw it. Did you post the video?

Maybe. It was recent where it was visible. Maybe that's partly how you found me.

I think so. Yes. I had never seen the video and it's so cool.

The organization I run is called We LOVE Arabian Horses. It's an independent, agnostic promoter of Arabian horses. We're a non-profit, a 501(c)(3). We do things that help expose and cause more people to learn about Arabian horses through outreach and educational programs. We post all kinds of people and pictures, everything from little kids—we don't know who they are, but there are some lovely pictures of children and Arabian horses, or older citizens and Arabian horses.

Some of them include some celebrities—like the horse from the movie *The Black Stallion* is an Arabian horse. The whole story is about an Arabian horse. *The Black Stallion*, when he was cast in the movie, it was a horse we're all very friendly with and one in fact a very close friend of mine owned. That horse's name is Cass Ole. When we put up photos of Cass Ole, *The Black Stallion*, and all that, people love, love, love, stories about Cass Ole. He's also long-since-deceased.

So people really enjoy hearing all about these stories from these more famous people. He [Cass Ole] was also owned by a Texas family. That would have been during Patrick's era; they would have been somewhat visible during the same time frames. I don't know what year *Dirty Dancing* was made versus what year *The Black Stallion* [1979] the movie was made.

A lot of us, including Patrick maybe, one way we all as children first got exposed to Arabian horses was the book *The Black Stallion*. That's written by a man named Walter Farley. Walter was also very, very visible in the Arabian horse community and he has died. His children are still carrying out his legacy. They would have circulated around that same time frame that Patrick was very visible.

Did you want to say anything else about your organization We LOVE Arabian Horses?

Our job is to help show and share the beauty and athleticism and personality of the Arabian horse to newcomers of all ages, and we do that through social media and in-person events, locally and globally. Our job is to introduce the horse to more and more folks.

Certainly, Patrick and other celebrities in our crowd are appealing attributes in the community.

When did you found the organization?

The brand was started in 2017 and it became a 501(c)(3) in 2022. We operate globally now. We have a very large online presence and then we create ambassadors around the USA and around the world who earn points for prizes to do things that put the Arabian horse in libraries and school programs, and take them to career days, and colleges, and give the Arabian horse exposure in multiple ways, other than coming to a horse show. We take the Arabian horse to them, wherever they are, whether it's kids in third grade and they've invited you to come in and bring the Arabian. We let people have fun ways to experience the Arabian horse through some type of touch event, like come sit on my Arabian horse or come have a little lesson, those kinds of things.

It's so wonderful that you do all that. It sounds like a wonderful organization.

It is. It's really the only one of its kind in terms of the way we do what we do. People very much enjoy it and love it.

I guarantee if Patrick was alive today, he would want to be involved with it in some way to help it grow and give more exposure to the Arabian horse.

I'm sure he would. I definitely agree with you.

We call those things "outreach events." Patrick, back in his day, did a lot of outreach events. I don't know that he necessarily thought of it that way back then, but it was like having the Arabian horse at a charity fundraising auction and Patrick would be the one who donated the horse to be sold at the auction.

He did those kind of things very, very much back in the day. Obviously, given his stardom and celebrity status, he could attract quite a crowd.

I don't know if many people are aware that he did those things.

The people down in Texas knew because we saw him more. He grew up in Houston. So all of us who grew up in the Houston area would see Patrick from kind of the beginning, and the McNair family and Gleannloch Farms, they're right out of Houston. So that Texas concentric circle would see Patrick a lot more frequently. And then over time, we started going to bigger events and farther away, like the national championships at that time were held in Louisville, Kentucky—and Patrick would be there.

We would normally mostly show our horses during the year, closer to home. Once you qualify, you go to the national championships and you can compete there in Kentucky. I think the industry has changed a little bit today, where we all go to events much farther away more commonly throughout the year. Back then, you would stay closer to home and show in the Houston or Texas area, like Dallas or Fort Worth, or San Antonio, and Patrick would be in those shows with us. The industry has just shifted a little bit.

I think he was a very busy person.

Yes.

LILLI KEELS

Arabian Horse Enthusiast

Written by Lilli Keels: 2017

My very first memory of Patrick and Donny was of them riding through our neighborhood on their bicycles. They weren't yet teenagers. I was younger than them, but my brothers were their ages.

Years later, Patrick was showing his Arabian in Houston at the Galleria. My brothers and I were on the third level when we noticed him and they started yelling "Tights" (a nickname they had given him because after football practice, he would wait until everyone left the locker room and would change into his dance tights before heading over to his mother's dance studio).

Patrick was showing his Arabian horse, but he started getting distracted looking all over the place for who was yelling. We kept running in different spots yelling it.

Patrick finally got a glimpse of us and motioned for us to come down and meet him. I think that's when I fell in love with Arabians, because two weeks later, I bought my first Arabian and my love for them continues!

MORE ABOUT PATRICK AND ARABIAN HORSES

"To the Arabian horse community, he was an accomplished and giving horseman. An active participant at Arabian shows throughout the late '80s and early '90s, Swayze's star power helped bring attention to the Arabian breed. Swayze's true passion for the horse earned him the utmost respect in the horse community."

From an article by Sarah Evers Conrad, September 15, 2009

"We at the Arabian Horse Association and our some 35,000 members mourn the loss of a great American icon, Patrick Swayze," said Lance Walters, Arabian Horse Association President. "He was an ardent lover of the Arabian horse and his passion for the breed would always spill over into the audience when he showed the beautiful horses—particularly with young people. His close friends called him 'Buddy' and that sentiment seemed to define his character, as I always found him to be a man of significant humility and grace. The Arabian horse has lost a dear friend and our prayers go out to his wife Lisa and family, and everyone who loved him. His significant contributions to the Arabian horse will not be forgotten."

From a Horsetalk.co.nz article, September 14, 2009

CHAPTER 8

PERFORMANCE NOTES: MORE AMAZING INFORMATION

1. Patrick Swayze performed in thirty-three cinema movies (from 1979–2009), six TV movies, and seven Broadway shows. He had numerous TV roles in multiple series and did countless TV appearances as himself.
2. Patrick performed songs (most written or co-written by Patrick) in five of his movies: *Dirty Dancing, Road House, Next of Kin, The Fox and the Hound 2*, and *One Last Dance*. His most popular song is "She's Like the Wind" which was co-written by Patrick and Stacy Widelitz (originally for *Grandview, U. S. A.*) and ultimately performed by Patrick, featuring Wendy Fraser, in the movie *Dirty Dancing*.
3. Patrick's dance career included performing with the Houston Jazz Ballet Company, the Buffalo Ballet, the Harkness Ballet, the Joffrey Ballet Company, and the Eliot Feld Ballet Company.
4. Patrick appeared in multiple music videos including: Ja Rule: "Murder Reigns" (2003) as an actor; Toto: "Rosanna" (1982) as a dancer, along with Cynthia Rhodes, who co-starred with him in *Dirty Dancing*; and Garth Brooks: "We Shall Be Free" (1993).
5. *North and South* was one of the most popular TV miniseries and also one of the most costly to make ($25 million) per the article in the *LA Times:* "'North and South' Rises Again" by Jane Sumner, February 27, 1994. (The article is focused on the three books written by John Jakes that were turned into a three-part TV miniseries and reports on why Patrick did not appear in Book Three.)
6. For *Dirty Dancing* (1987), Patrick had to downplay his dance skills to play the role of dance instructor Johnny Castle—except, of course, for the last scene.
7. In multiple interviews, Patrick talked about being offered anywhere

from $6-10 million dollars to do a sequel to *Dirty Dancing*, and he turned down the offers.
8. For *Road House* (1989), Patrick trained for the fight scenes with Benny Urquidez, a kick-boxing champion and action star. Urquidez thought so much of Patrick's skills that he suggested Patrick become a competitive kickboxer. Urquidez used Michael Jackson music to train Patrick, due to his dance background.
9. Patrick had to read almost the entire script during his audition for *Ghost*, but by the end of the reading, he had everyone there in tears.
10. *Ghost* was the highest grossing film of 1990.
11. In *Point Break* (1991), Keanu Reeves (as the character Johnny Utah) mentions a restaurant called "Patrick's Roadhouse" where Bodhi (Patrick) and one of his bank robbers have lunch. There actually was a real restaurant with that name at 106 Entrada Drive, Santa Monica, California. It closed in April 2024 after operating since 1973.
12. Patrick and Tammen (his favorite horse) won Grand Champion at the Nationals in 1993.
13. Patrick stayed at the historic Hotel Colorado in Glenwood Springs, Colorado, while filming *Tall Tale* (1995). His picture and autograph still hang in the main lobby. (Confirmed March 1, 2024 by Larry MacDonald, general manager of the hotel.)
14. Patrick Swayze talked about donating to charity some of the clothing he wore as a drag queen in *To Wong Foo, Thanks for Everything! Julie Newmar* (1995).
15. Patrick and his wife Lisa starred together, along with George de la Pena, in the dance movie *One Last Dance* (2003). The movie was directed by Lisa, who also wrote the screenplay. *One Last Dance* is based on the original 1984 play *Without A Word*, which Patrick and Lisa co-wrote and starred in with Nicholas Gunn. *Without A Word* won six LA Drama Critic Awards. Patrick described the movie as being a story about the concert dance world from the perspective of the dancers. The film also includes the theme that it is never too late to realize your dreams.
16. Patrick shared in a 2005 interview with the Official Patrick Swayze International Fan Club that he had a 200-year forest stewardship plan for his New Mexico ranch that he planned on accomplishing in twenty

years, and that he already had made significant progress.

17. When Patrick was starring in the musical *Guys and Dolls* in London (2006), *Dirty Dancing: The Classic Story on Stage* was playing across the street.
18. When Patrick was shooting the television series *The Beast* in Chicago (2009), the *Dirty Dancing* stage show was also playing there. Patrick told the *Chicago Tribune* that one day while filming *The Beast*, he was crossing the street as his character Barker, and he saw two cabs with ads for the *Dirty Dancing* stage show.
19. Patrick made a surprise appearance to open the first Stand Up to Cancer television fundraising broadcast, which was at the Kodak Theater on September 5, 2008. He received a standing ovation. He gave an elegant speech asking people to stand up to cancer with him. He said that people working together could make "a world where cancer does not mean living with fear, without hope, or worse."
20. On May 16, 2009, Patrick was awarded Best International Actor at the Monaco Film Festival in Monte Carlo for his role as Richard Pressburger in the movie *Jump!* (2007).
21. Jake Gyllenhaal had many tattoos (temporary, custom-made) put on him to honor Patrick while he was starring in the 2024 *Road House* remake.

Excerpts From the Official Patrick Swayze International Fan Club Website

From: Amazing Facts Every True Fan Should Know!!
[22.] Patrick really did drive the truck in *Black Dog*!

From: Frequently Asked Questions
[23.] Question to Patrick: How do you deal with being famous?
Patrick: "It was very difficult and confusing at first, but I have spent so many years learning the limitations of this particular lifestyle that I don't even think about it now."

[24.] Question to Patrick: Which co-star(s) has Patrick enjoyed working with the most through the years?
Patrick: "Mikey—my horse in *Tall Tale*!!" [Then Patrick went on to name three co-stars of the "human persuasion."]

CURTAIN CLOSER

I think the best way to close is to take heart from Patrick's words. Since at least 1988, Patrick spoke about the power of love and his desire for his work to enrich people's lives.

"It's not the history making movies that is the reason I've had a thirty-year career—it's much longer than a thirty-year career when you think I came out of the womb on the stage! I've always had an uncanny knack, whether it's a small movie or not, to find those characters, to find those roles even if they are dark characters to leave you out at the other end—that's changed you in some way, or seeing things in another way, or some level of identification that gets people to look from a different point of view. Usually, I like it to be something that has to do with heart. . . ."

Patrick Swayze, November 27, 2005, From interview by the Official Patrick Swayze International Fan Club

As for an example about heart, Patrick talks about playing the character of "drifter" Jack McCloud in *Three Wishes* (1995):

"If he's magical, he's only magical because he's a being that has to come from the heart."

"I'm really proud of this film because of the kind of heart it has. It's a four hanky movie. It definitely will break your heart and heal it, all in an hour-and-a-half, or at least give you the opportunity to heal your own heart. I feel it's a very responsible film from the point of view of not forcing emotion out of an audience. It's just a beautiful story about people trying to heal their lives and magic happening in this little boy's life and leaves the question mark: Did the magic really happen or did these people create it on their own because of their needs?"

Patrick Swayze, 1995, From Bobbie Wygant interview

Similar to Patrick speaking about the spiritual message of *Ghost* to Alex Simon in 2004, Patrick talks about this same wisdom in his movie *Three Wishes* to *Us Weekly* in 1995:

"It's about how the only thing we have is love . . . and that's all you take with you when you die."

Patrick Swayze, September 1995, From Tom O'Neill interview for Us Weekly

Credit: CBS Photo Archive/CBS via Getty Images.

From the 1990 movie Ghost, *Patrick Swayze as Sam Wheat and Demi Moore as Molly Jensen, in this famous tear-jerker, good-bye scene. Sam (as a ghost) leaves Molly, taking the love with him as he goes into "The Light."*

MY APPLAUSE

From the deepest part of my heart, I thank the many, many people who provided support, love, time, and expertise that greatly helped me write this book.

I thank with deep gratitude my family, especially my mom, Phyllis Friedman, and my dad, David Tabashnik—both of whom are always with me in spirit and who always encouraged me to be an avid reader throughout childhood and supported my ventures as an author. A very special shout-out goes to my brother, Bruce Tabashnik, who helped out with critical feedback and financial support of the book. David Tabashnik, my late brother, is always in my heart and I will never forget his support of me as an author. Special acknowledgment goes to my aunts, Mary Lou Zieve and Nedra Kapetansky, who were with me every step of the way. I also thank my nephew, Gabe Tabashnik, and my sister-in-law, Andrea Mathias.

A very special shout-out goes to my dear friend, Mary Kiriazis, for her unwavering support.

I thank my dear friend, Joshua Sinclair, for his friendship, support, and overall assistance with the book, including the tribute, photos, and review.

I thank my dear friend, Margaret, for her friendship; her work as president of the Official Patrick Swayze International Fan Club; permission to use material from the club's website and magazine; and getting me off to my real beginning as an author by asking me to write for the club magazine.

I know Bob Howell and Lee Santiwan are with me in spirit, and now, a fifth book.

I thank my dear friend, Jackie Horner, for supporting my writing and all of the *Dirty Dancing* stories—you are greatly missed.

I am very grateful to my book designer extraordinaire, Patricia Bacall, and editors extraordinaire, Pamela Cangioli and Kimberley Jace.

I thank my expert attorneys, Carolyn Schurr Levin and Joe Perry.

I gratefully thank Steve Harrison and his team, especially Cristina Smith, Gail Snyder, Joe McAllister, and Claire Doney, at Author Success, for their marketing and publicity programs, and classes.

I thank my team for helping me keep on the path, especially Dr. Yashinsky, Dr. Wermers, Dr. A., Rochelle, and John Gifford.

I deeply acknowledge the generosity and graciousness of the interviewees and contributors for the sharing of their memories, stories, tributes, photos, material, and time: Joe Leydon, Alex Simon, Joshua Sinclair, Eleanor Bergstein, Linda Gottlieb, Jaclyn Smith, Timothy Linh Bui, Elliott Sharp, Jordan Brady, Vincent Angell, Christopher Riordan, Terri Garber, Marshall Teague, BoJesse Christopher, John Philbin, Larry Ward, Frank Whiteley, Jeff Healey, Steve Newton, Bruce Morrow, Denise Amirante, Bill EuDaly, Melissa Perry, Scott Wilder, Tom Sanders, Ray Cottingham, Patrick Youngblood, Amy Osborn, Joe Cervantez, Michael Porterfield, Mike Hammond, Glenn Watkins, Dwight Baxter, Rachel M. Leon, Michael Pascoe, Vicki Mancuso, Nancy Schmidt, Francie Mendenhall, Heather Sparacino Crane, Katherin Kovin-Pacino, Jan Griffith, Crystal L. Berger, Claire Gregan, Regine, Paul Kostial, Lilli Keels, Bobbie Wygant/Bobbie Wygant Archives, and Sarah Evers Conrad.

I send a big thank-you to Timothy Linh Bui for the photos, advance read, feedback, and review.

I send a big thank-you to Linda and Jeff Michael for their friendship and support of the book.

I send a big thank-you to Peter Iliff for referring me to John Philbin and BoJesse Christopher.

I send a big thank-you to Rena Jacobs for her assistance with the Jaclyn Smith interview excerpt.

I send a big thank-you to Martha McClintock at Getty Images.

I send a big thank-you to Rob and Pam Hess for use of Rob's classic photo of Patrick and Tammen.

I send a big thank-you to Hopper Stone, SMPSP, for *Green Dragon* images.

I send a big thank-you to Justine Rigos and Alex Kerbabian at Shutterstock.

I send a big thank-you to these people from the Arabian horse world: Robin Marshall, editor of *Horsetalk.co.nz* for use of material from the magazine; Glenye Oakley for use of material from a USEF article; and to Cindy Johnson, sales manager, Sam Houston Race Park, for facilitating use of quotes from the Bob Bork interview of Patrick (with Tammen).

I send a big thank-you to the following media for permission to use their material: Alan Gibbons, editor-in-chief, *Orange Coast* magazine; the BBC; Erik Clapp from the Bobbie Wygant Archives; and Patricia Gonzalez for *Us Weekly*.

Special thanks to Roger Costa from the estate of Jeff Healey for appreciation of the use of Steve Newton's Jeff Healey interview excerpt. Special thanks to David Donnelly, brother of Kevin Donnelly, for permission to use the *Point Break* photo. Special thanks to Simone Don for running the Dancing Dragon World YouTube videos. Special thanks to Larry MacDonald, general manager at Hotel Colorado.

I gratefully thank the readers of my books and the fans of Patrick, including my Patrick Facebook friends and the administrators of Patrick-related Facebook groups, for keeping Patrick's memory and legacy alive.

PERMISSIONS

All of the contributors in this book gave permission for the tributes they wrote and the telephone and email interviews conducted by the author to be used in this book.

I gratefully thank all of the contributors and sources for giving me permission to use their memories, stories, and tributes in this homage to Patrick.

CHAPTER ONE

"No matter how much": © 1988 by Joe Leydon. "Patrick Swayze: Back in Houston." The Moving Picture Show with Joe Leydon (movingpictureshow.com). December 19, 1988.

"But I really am hellbent": © 1995 by Joe Leydon. "Patrick Swayze: Getting in touch with his feminine side as a most womanly woman in 'To Wong Foo.'" The Moving Picture Show with Joe Leydon (movingpictureshow.com). September 3, 1995.

"Patrick fashioned his own": © 2017 by Sue Tabashnik. *PATRICK SWAYZE The Dreamer* by Sue Tabashnik. Passion Spirit Dreams Press. 2017. Used with permission of Joshua Sinclair.

"I have been fortunate enough": © 2009 by Joshua Sinclair. Written by and used with permission of Joshua Sinclair. Previously published in *PATRICK SWAYZE The Dreamer* by Sue Tabashnik. Passion Spirit Dreams Press. 2017.

"People have said many": © 2017 by Sue Tabashnik. *PATRICK SWAYZE The Dreamer* by Sue Tabashnik. Passion Spirit Dreams Press. 2017. Written by and used with permission of Eleanor Bergstein.

"Patrick had a really": © 2013 by Sue Tabashnik. Interview of Linda Gottlieb in *The Fans Love Story ENCORE: How the Movie* DIRTY DANCING *Captured the Hearts of Millions!* by Sue Tabashnik. Passion Spirit Dreams Press. 2013. (Edited November 4, 2016.) Used with permission of Linda Gottlieb.

"Yes. And I knew her children": © 2022 by Sue Tabashnik. Interview of Jaclyn Smith in *Patsy Swayze: Every Day, A Chance to Dance* by Sue Tabashnik. Passion Spirit Dreams Press. 2022. Used with permission of Jaclyn Smith.

"Yes. [According to Elliott Sharp]": © 2013 by Vice Media. "Patrick Swayze-The Lost Tapes." Elliott Sharp. (Vice.com). April 11, 2013.

"Patrick was a dear man": © 2017 by Sue Tabashnik. *PATRICK SWAYZE The Dreamer* by Sue Tabashnik. Passion Spirit Dreams Press. 2017. Written by and used with permission of Jordan Brady.

"Patrick was always": Used with permission of the Official Patrick Swayze International Fan Club from their interview of Jordan Brady in 2000. Used with permission of Jordan Brady.

"Working with Patrick Swayze": © 2017 by Sue Tabashnik. *PATRICK SWAYZE The Dreamer* by Sue Tabashnik. Passion Spirit Dreams Press. 2017. Written by and used with permission of Marshall Teague.

"Yeah, '91": © by Sue Tabashnik. Interview of Frank Whiteley in *Patsy Swayze: Every Day, A Chance to Dance* by Sue Tabashnik. Passion Spirit Dreams Press. 2022. Used with permission of Frank Whiteley.

CHAPTER TWO

"What saved me was": "Patrick Swayze *Black Dog*." Used with permission from the archives of bobbiewygant.com. Bobbie Wygant, a long-time entertainment reporter and critic with NBC 5 KXAS-TV Channel 5 Dallas/Fort Worth. 1998.

"I come from a place": © 2004 by *Venice Magazine*. "PATRICK SWAYZE: PEACEFUL WARRIOR." Alex Simon. June 2004. Re-published June 10, 2015 in "Great Conversations: Patrick Swayze." Alex Simon, Co-editor. The Hollywood Interview. (https://thehollywoodinterview.blogspot.com).

"This is my keepsake": © 1995 by *Us Weekly LLC*. "Patrick Swayze-The US Interview." September 1995. Tom O'Neill. All rights reserved. Used with permission.

"He's a marvellous individual": © 1988 by Steve Newton. "That Time I Asked 22-Year-Old Jeff Healey what Patrick Swayze was like to work with on *Road House*." Steve Newton. Earofnewt.com. July 1, 1988.

"It is a BIG deal": © 2017 by Sue Tabashnik. *PATRICK SWAYZE The Dreamer* by Sue Tabashnik. Passion Spirit Dreams Press. 2017. (Edited March 13, 2023.) Written by and used with permission of Tom Sanders.

"I'll tell you about Buddy": © 2010 by Sue Tabashnik. Interview of Michael Porterfield in *The Fans' Love Story: How the Movie* DIRTY DANCING *Captured the Hearts of Millions!* by Sue Tabashnik. Outskirts Press. 2010. Used with permission of Michael Porterfield.

CHAPTER THREE

"That's the other side": © 2004 by *Venice Magazine*. "PATRICK SWAYZE: PEACEFUL WARRIOR." Alex Simon. June 2004. Re-published June 10, 2015 in "Great Conversations: Patrick Swayze." Alex Simon, Co-editor. The Hollywood Interview. (https://thehollywoodinterview.blogspot.com).

"Patrick: I was literally born": BBC. *HARDtalk Extra*. Gavin Esler. 2006. Used with permission from BBC.

"I went to Purchase College": © 2022 by Sue Tabashnik. Interview of Dwight Baxter in *Patsy Swayze: Every Day, A Chance to Dance* by Sue Tabashnik. Passion Spirit Dreams Press. 2022. Used with permission of Dwight Baxter.

"After we finished the major push": Used with permission of the Official Patrick Swayze International Fan Club. Interview of Patrick Swayze. November 27, 2005.

CHAPTER FOUR

"He really taught me": © 2004 by *Venice Magazine*. "PATRICK SWAYZE: PEACEFUL WARRIOR." Alex Simon. June 2004. Re-published June 10, 2015 in "Great Conversations: Patrick Swayze." Alex Simon, Co-editor. The Hollywood Interview. (https://thehollywoodinterview.blogspot.com).

"I met Patsy's son, Patrick/Buddy": © 2022 by Sue Tabashnik. Interview of Francie Mendenhall in *Patsy Swayze: Every Day, A Chance to Dance* by Sue Tabashnik. Passion Spirit Dreams Press. 2022. (Edited May 11, 2023.) Used with permission of Francie Mendenhall.

"Patsy was fun and energetic": © 2022 by Sue Tabashnik. Interview of Katherin Kovin-Pacino in *Patsy Swayze: Every Day, A Chance to Dance* by Sue Tabashnik. Passion Spirit Dreams Press. 2022. Used with permission of Katherin Kovin-Pacino.

CHAPTER FIVE

"Swayze and his wife": © 1988 by Joe Leydon. "Patrick Swayze: Back in Houston." The Moving Picture Show with Joe Leydon (movingpictureshow.com). December 19, 1988.

"Sam Elliott (*Mask, Murder in Texas*)": © 1989 by Joe Leydon. "Patrick Swayze on 'Road House.'" The Moving Picture Show with Joe Leydon (movingpictureshow.com). May 14, 1989.

"Goodbye, Patrick": © 2004 by *Venice Magazine*. "PATRICK SWAYZE: PEACEFUL WARRIOR." Alex Simon. June 2004. Re-published June 10, 2015 in "Great Conversations: Patrick Swayze." Alex Simon, Co-editor. The Hollywood Interview. (https://thehollywoodinterview.blogspot.com).

"Patrick Swayze has always": © 2004 by *Venice Magazine*. "PATRICK SWAYZE: PEACEFUL WARRIOR." Alex Simon. Ibid.

CHAPTER SIX

"Fans have been so faithful": © 2004 by *Orange Coast* magazine. "Power of One." Greg Hernandez. July 2004 (Volume 30, Number 7).

"Summer of 1989": © 2010 by Sue Tabashnik. Written by and used with permission of Crystal L. Berger. *The Fans' Love Story: How the Movie* DIRTY DANCING *Captured the Hearts of Millions!* by Sue Tabashnik. Outskirts Press. 2010.

"When I was a six-year-old girl": © 2010 by Sue Tabashnik. Written by and used with permission of Claire Gregan. *The Fans' Love Story: How the Movie* DIRTY DANCING *Captured the Hearts of Millions!* by Sue Tabashnik. Outskirts Press. 2010.

CHAPTER SEVEN

"I grew up with horses": © 2009 by Horsetalk.co.nz. "Arabian horse breeder and actor Patrick Swayze dies." September 14, 2009.

"I have a real passion": © 1997. Sam Houston Race Park. From a video hosted by Bob Bork at the Sam Houston Race Park, September 13, 1997.

"To the Arabian horse": © 2009 by USEF (United States Equestrian Federation.) "Arabian Horse Enthusiast Patrick Swayze Dies at 57." Sarah Evers Conrad. September 15, 2009.

"We at the Arabian": © 2009 by Horsetalk.co.nz. "Arabian horse breeder and actor Patrick Swayze dies." September 14, 2009.

CHAPTER EIGHT

"16. Patrick shared in": Used with permission of the Official Patrick Swayze International Fan Club. Interview of Patrick Swayze. November 27, 2005.

"Excerpts From the Official": Used with permission of the Official Patrick Swayze International Fan Club. F.A.Q. AMAZING FACTS EVERY FAN SHOULD KNOW!! (http://www.patrickswayze.net/fanclub.htm).

CURTAIN CLOSER

"It's not the history": Used with permission of the Official Patrick Swayze International Fan Club. Interview of Patrick Swayze. November 27, 2005.

"If he's magical,": "Patrick Swayze *Three Wishes*." Used with permission from the archives of bobbiewygant.com. Bobbie Wygant, a long-time entertainment reporter and critic with NBC 5 KXAS-TV Channel 5 Dallas/Fort Worth. 1995.

"It's about how": © 1995 by *Us Weekly LLC*. "Patrick Swayze-The US Interview." September 1995. Tom O'Neill. All rights reserved. Used with permission which includes use on the back cover and in the interior of the book.

ABOUT THE AUTHOR

Sue Tabashnik is a critically acclaimed author of five books about Patrick Swayze, Patsy Swayze, and the movie *Dirty Dancing*. She became an avid fan of Patrick Swayze in 1988. She was a very active member of the Official Patrick Swayze International Fan Club from 2000–2010, which included writing numerous articles for the club magazine. She had the good fortune to meet Patrick Swayze and some of his family at movie screenings and benefit events, and this changed her life forever.

Credit: Murray Goldenberg.

Sue has interviewed or talked with hundreds of people connected to Patrick Swayze and has done extensive media research. She was the special guest speaker at the *Dirty Dancing* Festival in Lake Lure, North Carolina in 2018 and has done multiple radio shows and podcasts. Several of her books have received awards; most recently, *Patsy Swayze: Every Day, A Chance to Dance* won first place in the performing arts category in the 2024 Book Excellence Awards.

Sue worked as a master's level social worker from 1977–2022, which included conducting thousands of interviews. She has lived most of her life in the Detroit area.

Author website: https://www.likedirtydancing.com

www.ingramcontent.com/pod-product-compliance
Lightning Source LLC
Chambersburg PA
CBHW040551010526
44110CB00054B/2632